The Therafields Psychotherapy Community

Promise, Betrayal, and Demise

Brenda M. Doyle

BRENDA M DOYLE PHD

tellwell

Tellwell Talent
www.tellwell.ca

ISBN
978-0-2288-3932-3 (Paperback)
978-0-2288-3936-1 (eBook)

To my daughters Elizabeth and Catherine, my
grandchildren Theo, Emily, and Billie, and to Peter

Table of Contents

Preface 1

Introduction 5

Lea Hindley-Smith 9

Therapy in 1966-67 19

The Marathon at Bigwin Resort 26

The Farm 30

An Early Warning Sign 33

A New Administration 36

Meeting Visvaldis 43

Return From North Carolina 46

The Willow, Harry, and Visvaldis 51

Lea's Life and Roles Post-North Carolina 57

'Threshold Therapy' 63

The Character Analysis Group (CAG) 70

At the Farm: 1970-73 77

At the Willow 85

The Learning Groups 89

Regarding Homosexuality 102

Other 'Health' interventions and 'Teachings' 106

Families and Children 111

Lea and her Children 117

'Work Therapy' 127

The Summer of Discontent: 1975 132

The Therafields' School 140

Having Children 146

Ka School 153

Lea, Visvaldis, and the Environmental Centre 159

The End of Ka School 161

Lea and her 'Caretakers' in the Late 1970s Onward 171

Toward the End 180

The Dissolution of Therafields 184

Conclusion 189

Epilogue 1: Another Look at Intentional Communities
of the 1960s and 1970s 195

Epilogue 2: Another Communal Example,
Another Cautionary Tale 197

Bibliography 201

Acknowledgements 203

About the Author 205

Preface

My introduction to the community that would become known as Therafields began one day in July 1966 when I met with Lea Hindley-Smith, its core founder, to talk about my need for counselling. Though I was excited about meeting her, I could have had no sense of the radical importance of that interview for the whole of my life. Nor could Lea at that moment in her career have foretold the directions that she would take within the next few years that would in some ways turn inside out the values her early work had embodied. Both of us were moving along an arc of our own. I badly longed for connection, for understanding, for a solid base on which to anchor my young adult self. Lea, however, was reaching the outer limits of her capacity to provide that base for the by-then scores of young people seeking her help. Over the next seventeen years, I lived within the community known as Therafields. Lea and I both changed a great deal between 1966 and 1983 in ways related to our own inner struggles and desires, as well as to the directions taken in the community itself.

By 1983 I was taking undergraduate courses in psychology, preparatory for the graduate school which I entered a year later. I was also leaving a 14-year relationship with my husband whom I had met and married within the community. These events precipitated my leaving behind the already disintegrating entity of Therafields. The close friendships that I had developed during those years remained steady, however. If anything, they have deepened and grown in the intervening years. Over the following fourteen years I received my doctorate in psychology, did a bit of teaching at Ryerson and York Universities and some consulting, spent a year as an intern at the Clarke Institute, became registered as a psychologist, and developed a private practice. Throughout, somewhere at the back of my

1

mind remained unresolved questions about the nature and history of the Therafields community, and about my own 17-year odyssey within what had been for me a second family.

In the fall of 1997 I began a series of interviews with forty-seven people who had belonged to Therafields. I taped and transcribed each interview. My original idea had been to obtain material about Therafields for a magazine article. The project gradually developed into thoughts of a book that would not only look at the community itself, but also would set it within the broader context of the zeitgeist of the 1960s. But by the spring of 1998 I had had enough of the project. I was then too busy with other work to devote the time needed to do it justice. Besides, I realized that the deeper reason for my research was an attempt to understand for myself what exactly had happened during the years 1966-83 while I was involved with the community. It seemed to me that I had lived in a large and complex extended family, a village almost. As I 'grew up' there I experienced and intuited changes that were happening around me but was unable to fully understand or articulate them. In my interviews, I had the opportunity to talk in some depth with people who had had different locations within the community, often with quite different experiences. Out of this period of research I began to understand more what had been happening with myself and others, and, how the various pieces related to one another.

In preparation for the publication of this manuscript, I connected with my respondents for whom I have contact information to ask their wishes regarding anonymity. A desire not to be directly quoted or mentioned is strong. In the digital age any reference to an individual can become public knowledge. Those with whom I have spoken are fine with my using their thoughts and experiences but generally wish to remain anonymous. They realize that in most cases people from the community will recognize their voices or stories, but are unconcerned about that eventuality. Thus, in this text I refer directly only to people who have given me permission to do so, or those who have passed away. For those who have asked for anonymity, I have placed the word 'pseudonym' after the name I have given to them. In a few cases when I have been unable to reach someone, I have simply given a first name and an initial, particularly when the comment reveals no personal information. In others, I have spoken of, for example, 'one man' or 'one woman' who told me something. An exception to this rule is regarding Lea's children, whose roles and impact upon the community were of a piece with Lea's own. I refer directly to them, both in the things that they told me in my interviews with them and in the experiences of others and myself in relation to them.

Introduction

Therafields was the product of several threads coalescing during an historical period that favoured new, even revolutionary directions taken by young people. In the 1960s and 1970s there was an exponential mushrooming of groups founding communities based on similar values and interests. Timothy Miller's book *The 60s Communes: Hippies and Beyond*, studies intentional communities in the United States which, before 1960, numbered in the hundreds. In the 1960s an explosion of communal living took that number to thousands, even as he states, to tens of thousands. These communities varied considerably in numbers, locations, and underlying values. Their most common feature was however, a preponderance of young, white people of middle-class background. Thousands of the groups were religious in nature – many, for example, "Jesus hippie groups" that blended counter-cultural ideals with aspects of Christianity. There were Jewish communes and ones founded on the beliefs of Asian religions like Buddhism that were beginning to make inroads in the USA. But there were also thousands based on secular values: political commitment – often leftist, or, working for social change – for example, running shelters for the homeless. Other groups were actively against political involvement, preferring experimentation with drugs and freedom from responsibility. Agitation for the rights of homosexuals led to the creation of some communal settings, especially for lesbians. Some were focused on the arts, while others were devoted to medicine, therapy, or personal growth. Environmentalism was a large component of intentional communities in that era, as consciousness of the impact of humanity upon the planet grew. In urban settings, there were groups that focused on the provision of affordable and congenial housing, a trend reawakening today with the growing interest in co-housing.

Miller and other sociologists in the United States studying the communal movement during the 1960s have noted a variety of themes prevalent in that lifestyle. One was a critique of the plastic nature of modern life, a movement away from "the natural." Some groups advocated nudity as a valuing of the human body, a way to let go of shame often associated in the past with the body and its functions. Meals in common were stressed as places for deeper conversations and acquaintance. Debates over the consumption of foods like refined sugars or of meats were often found to occur. Some communes, especially ones founded from the perspective of a religion, maintained a regimen of dietary restrictions. In some places, the acceptance of multiple sexual partners led to spells of sexually-transmitted diseases, though Miller points out that the degree to which communes were credited with open sexual activity, has been greatly exaggerated. Similarly, the assumption that all communes were centres of hedonistic, drug-centred behaviour, was false. Some certainly had that focus, but many more did not.

In the 1960s there was a sense of idealism abroad especially among youth. Books rejecting materialism and seeking higher consciousness found willing readers on university campuses. It was the era of civil rights. John Kennedy invited young people to look beyond themselves, to do something for their country, to join the Peace Corps. Television exposed abuses perpetrated on black people in the South seeking civil rights, as well as on the Vietnamese people by the US army. Moreover, that war itself demanded that young men accept being drafted into the army and sent abroad to join in the carnage.

There were similarities but also differences in the elements that brought the people who formed the Therafields community in the mid-60s and the 1970s to live together. In Canada, we were not as immediately impacted as were our contemporaries in the USA by the 1950s threats of the Cold War and the possibilities of nuclear attacks. But as television became a normalized feature of daily life, we also participated in American political and cultural life. Our parents were people who had grown up during the Depression and who had weathered the second World War. Stability and conservation were watchwords for them: get a job and keep it; get married and have a family; hold on to what you have. But coming of age in the 60s, we entered an expanding economy with an array of futures available.

6

We could afford to take risks and to explore areas specifically shunned by our parents. To that generation, talking about personal problems or family issues was taboo. Social security required that they be kept private. "What would the neighbours think?" was a phrase denoting serious consequences to the individual and to the family. But living in an urban setting where neighbours were essentially strangers, we didn't care too much about what they thought. Getting together with a therapist or in a therapy group where one could be open about one's struggles, was tremendously helpful. The idealism of the 60s affected us as it did those of our American contemporaries. As well, for those of us in the Catholic Church, Pope John XXIII and his Vatican Council of the early 1960s opened new windows of thought and personal freedom of choice.

It is possible that the Therafields community which flourished in Toronto from the mid-1960s to the early 1980s, is unique in its psychotherapeutic origins and focus. At its zenith the community comprised about a thousand people, many of whom lived communally in the 35 large houses in Toronto's Annex. In the country near Orangeville, Ontario, five farms and a former schoolhouse property were owned, managed, and lived in by community members. Two of these were substantially renovated and extended to provide accommodation for lengthy group meetings that occurred there with regularity. An organic garden, cared for by volunteers, produced food for the people who swelled the ranks of the regular farm group on weekends and during the summer. In the city four properties along Dupont Ave., were renovated to provide office space for individual therapists, as well as group rooms, bio-energetic rooms, and a restaurant that was also used as a locale for entertainment.

Therafields did not originate as an intentional community, however. Its starting point was the psychotherapy practice of Lea Hindley Smith, a gifted lay therapist who was self-educating even as her practice grew from humble origins in the mid-1950s. In 1964-6 her work mushroomed exponentially as theology students of Father Gregory Baum, himself a charismatic teacher and a respected theologian, entered her sphere, bringing along with them a host of other young people from St. Michael's College and beyond. The demands upon Lea's time and energy necessitated changes in methods and structures that set in place an organism entitled Therafields by the fall of 1967.

Throughout the 1970s and into the early 1980s this entity would evolve in ways that were of benefit to some and harmful to others. By the late 1970s Lea's physical and mental health had deteriorated to a point that she was becoming little more than a figurehead to the organization. In the early 1980s she suffered a psychotic breakdown and was hospitalized for some months. She never regained in any sense her presence and authority within the community. Financial difficulties and the discontent of the leading psychotherapists with the administration chaired by Lea's younger son, Rob, led to a gradual disintegration of the core of the institution in its properties and its seminar of therapists. In 1984 Lea's older son, Malcolm was arrested, convicted, and imprisoned for the sexual abuse of girls in the school for Therafields children that he had taken over in 1975. A community that had had in its early formation the hope and promise of healthy and productive lives for its adherents, came apart. By 1985 Therafields ceased to exist as an entity other than in its Foundation which carried on projects according to its charter for another decade or so. One other significant addendum however, is the training school started by some of the former seminar members and other non-Therafields colleagues in 1985, called the Centre For Training in Psychotherapy. It continues successfully to this day.

But for many who like myself were a part of the community for most or part of those years 1964-85, and for others who knew of the significant presence of Therafields within Toronto, especially in the Annex area of Toronto, and in the rural areas surrounding the farm, the question has persisted: what happened? What was going on within the organization, at one time so strong and forward looking, that brought it within two decades to its knees. This book is written to address that question.

Lea Hindley-Smith

At the point when I met her, Lea had been working with what at the time she called, as in the medical model, 'patients,' for over ten years. This work had come about as a gradual evolution, based upon the necessity of supporting her family, as well as her on-going interest in counselling and psychotherapy. It is no simple project to describe her early life. Contradictory statements made by Lea at different times to different people, as well as fragments thrown out in her writings, shadow what pieces we can glean. Clearly Lea constructed a past with a happy early childhood, loving parents, and a supportive extended family. This story, however, is belied by information that she disclosed to others in more private or vulnerable moments.

As Grant Goodbrand discovered in his research for his book, *Therafields: The Rise and Fall of Lea Hindley-Smith's Psychoanalytic Commune*, her birth in Cardiff, Wales was to a father of Baltic Jewish descent and a Jewish mother whose family members were professional people. Lea's father's family name had been Tannenzapf, but had been shortened to Tannen when they immigrated to England, later changed to Tanner by Lea. The family appears to have lived a secular life and it is not possible to know if any religious rituals were followed. Anti-Semitism in England, and indeed in most countries, would have negatively influenced Lea in her early life, likely explaining why she did not disclose her heritage but sought to evade issues of religious background even when asked directly.

Lea's father was a musician and a gambler. He was not an equal partner with his wife. Lea's only experience of a responsible man in her early life seems to have been her maternal grandfather. One of her deepest connections was with her 'nurse,' or nanny, who cared for her while her mother worked until Lea was eight. It is probable that the relationship between her parents was tempestuous during this period as when she was eight her mother separated from her father. The 'nurse,' so important to her left the family, and Lea's relationship with her father was severed. Her mother appears to have been either physically or emotionally unwell during this period though it seems that she was not supported by her own family in the crisis. Not too long after the separation, Lea's father was institutionalized with mental illness and was never released. His musical instruments were denied him and he died alone in the hospital about 16 years later. The circumstances of her father's death were traumatic for Lea and she would speak from time to time of a desire to prevent this fate from occurring to others. At some point in her youth, Lea's older sister died, as did her brother.

Lea left Cardiff and moved to London, working sometimes as an artist's model. She spoke of being a student nurse at the Great Ormond Street Hospital though it is doubtful that she completed the course as she never spoke of being a nurse or of working as one. The hospital has no record of her presence there as a student. At some point, she saw a psychotherapist named Mike at the British Psychoanalytic Association. She may or may not have taken courses in Freudian psychology, though it is likely that her interest in Freud was stimulated through her work with Mike, a therapist of whom she spoke with affection and respect.

Sometime before the outbreak of World War II, Lea met and married Harry Hindley-Smith, a textile worker from Yorkshire. Her later writings indicate that she entered the marriage on the rebound from another relationship that had ended badly. Harry was about 10 years older than Lea. He had confidence and stability that might have appealed to a young woman on her own in London. Their first child, Malcolm, was born in 1939. Early in the war when London was being blitzed, the couple moved to Yorkshire to be near Harry's family. While there, Lea worked outside the home and entrusted her son to other women with young children. Lea spoke well of Harry's family, especially his mother whom she found down-to-earth and warmly welcoming. While in Yorkshire, Lea met and learned hypnosis techniques from a former coal-miner who had been treated with this method after a serious accident. Her daughter, Josie, was born in 1945 and Rob about three years later.

After the war, the British economy was in disarray and Harry had trouble getting steady work. The couple decided to try their luck in Canada and moved here in 1948. The situation in Toronto was not much better, however, and Harry never again found work in his field. For some years the family seems to have survived on what Harry could scrape together from part-time work and on the sale of a series of houses that they would purchase, fix-up, and sell. Lea had a good eye for real estate potential and learned to make cosmetic changes that would increase the value of a house quickly. Her orientation was toward the large, and at the time undervalued, homes in Toronto's Annex. For some years Lea cared for her family and worked on house improvement. In England she had discovered a talent for talking with and counselling young people with whom she shared lodgings.

The houses in Toronto were large enough to take in boarders – a necessary source of income for the family – and Lea found herself again becoming involved in the lives of young people living with her. She tumbled to the fact that she was able to talk with and help them, sensing that she could make a career as a counsellor. By then she was menopausal, and it was clear that nothing much would change between Harry and her. She was very unsatisfied and had nowhere to put her considerable energies, so she started to work with people. She read psychological and therapeutic materials. She was a bright woman and she had enough background and emotional resources to handle it. She found her way doing it a little at a time. Earlier Lea had made money reading cards or tea leaves at parties. She advertised her talent in newspapers. Gradually a clientele developed. When she began to use hypnotism with clients, she advertised as a hypnotist. Over time the practice that grew became the focus of her life.

In the 1950s, like today, there was a variety of people who gave counsel to people needing help. Their degree of training and expertise varied and continues to vary greatly. A priest, minister, or rabbi, a teacher, a nurse or doctor, a friend of the family, an experienced relative, might be called upon. In more serious situations of mental health there were psychiatrists and in some communities, psychoanalysts. Today, though laws govern who can call themselves psychologists and psychotherapists, any person can be a counsellor, a life coach, or a fortune teller without recrimination, unless, of course, serious negative outcomes become public. Without evident qualifications, then as now, success within the broad sector of 'counselling' depends upon the personal qualities of the counsellor, and Lea's personal qualities were considerable. She was intelligent, insightful, and compassionate. She had a strong, at times commanding presence. She read the available literature on psychotherapy – especially at the beginning, by Freud, later by others of his colleagues, as well as more radical practitioners. She relied upon her own experiences to give grounded counsel, helping people to understand their problems and to move forward in their lives. She was very encouraging to her clients. Reading Freud's essay on lay therapists – people who could embarked on the work of psychoanalysis despite not being psychiatrists – a future that he envisioned – she begin to identify herself in that fashion.

In the late 1950s the Hindley-Smiths had a home on Madison Avenue. Later they moved to 152 Howland Avenue. A few of Lea's clients moved in as boarders. These were people about whom she had a special concern as they seemed to be living bleak and isolated lives. Her intention was for them to live together in a supportive manner, meeting with her from time to time to discuss how they were managing. The family lived separately. In 1961 while living there, Lea started her first therapy group, composed of people whom she saw regularly for individual sessions. Writing many years later in *Not For You Tea In The Afternoon,* she commented that bringing her clients together seemed a way to prevent their becoming too dependent and focused on her. This type of group was later designated a 'standard' group to distinguish it from 'house' and 'learning' groups. Lea's dining room table became the setting for each meeting. That first one was small – perhaps about eight people -- and was informal. Members would sometimes bring fruit or candy to share, or on special occasions, a celebratory bottle of liquor. Participants would speak of their troubles and support one another under Lea's guidance. In 1962 Lea and Harry bought and moved to 477 Brunswick Avenue. 152 Howland then became Lea's first house group as eight people moved in together, meeting as a group with her once a week. At 477 Brunswick Lea had her office in the front bedroom on the second floor. The downstairs living room was used as a waiting room and the dining room table served again for her groups. The following fall, the basement of 477 was fixed up and outfitted to become a group room.

Tom O'Sullivan first met Lea in May 1961. He was a Catholic seminarian who had already a masters' degree in psychology and had become registered. He was working for the Children's Aid Society, giving some lectures, and had a radio show on psychological matters. He heard about Lea through a fellow seminarian who was seeing her. Tom was leaving soon for another spate of courses at Wayne University in the USA but was interested to meet Lea nonetheless. He recalled,

> "It was astonishing. I was leaving on Monday and I saw her on Friday. We really hit it off. She was the first person I met who had read Freud and who saw him the way that I did. She invited me to come back for another talk on Sunday, but I said no because I knew that if I did, I wouldn't leave."

When he returned later to Toronto, Tom called Lea and began to see her as his therapist. "It was mind-boggling. I was learning so much," he said. He continued at the seminary, studying theology, teaching psychology, and seeing some of the seminarians who wanted his help. In the spring of 1963, after Tom had left the seminary, Lea asked him to take on some of her in-coming clients. By the same token, Tom was referring to her priests and seminarians whom he knew needed help. Tom remembered that by that time, "We were both swamped. I was seeing about 25 people."

Jerry Laughlin met Lea at 477 Brunswick in1964. He had been given her name by a priest that he knew.

> "Therafields didn't exist then. I just saw her one-on-one and she was wonderful. She was very fair about her fees. She was full of hope and I felt very encouraged. She pointed out lots of ways that I was holding myself back, all kinds of things that wouldn't have occurred to me in a million years. It was unbelievable. When she bought and moved over to 59 Admiral, I went into 477 Brunswick with others. It was a great house. I was there for two years. It was the beginning of really good friendships. They were all good people, good friends."

Meg K. (a pseudonym) came to see Lea in 1963 suffering from physical ailments that her doctor believed to have a psychological connection. A co-worker gave her Lea's phone number. She remembered,

> "Lea answered the phone in what seemed to me a rather irritating British accent. When I went to see her on Brunswick Avenue, she seemed a weird duck. I answered her questions thoughtfully but felt nothing. At the next session she used relaxation with me and my therapy began."

Meg went into one of Lea's groups the following month and later moved into 152 Howland with the others. A few people, called outriders, didn't live there but would visit, hang out with the house group members, and attend their weekly meetings with Lea. In the basement of the house where their kitchen and dining room were, two of Lea's long-time clients, Jack King and Gus O'Brien carried on what Meg spoke of as, "pretty much 24 hour a day therapy." Jack and Gus had both been seeing Lea for years. They were two of the people whom she had brought into her home at 152 Howland out of concern for the poverty of their social lives. In Meg's house group they were the more psychologically mature members who would be present for newer members to rely upon for grounding and for talking about feelings or their dreams as needed on a day-to-day basis. This was not something that Lea had necessarily advocated. It simply became a feature of the shared lives of people living a somewhat familial existence within a psycho-therapeutic context.

Meg realized when she came into therapy that Lea was beginning to deal with some pretty disturbed people in her Monday-Thursday group. In earlier groups, compared to what happened later, the work was more or less 'Micky Mouse.' In her early work Lea typically would ask a person why they had come to see her. Usually the issues would be relatively concrete: trouble with a boss, a partner, or with friends, a decision to be made, and so on. Lea would ask questions to get a sense of the parameters of the problem – who was involved; how long had it gone on; had this happened in other circumstances or with other people, etc. Making use of her own experience of life and relationships, the reading of psychological literature that she was doing, the therapy that she had herself had while in England, and importantly, allowing herself to get a sense of the person before her, Lea was able to rely on her intuitions to begin to formulate words, suggestions, encouragements that could help him or her with the problem presented.

I experienced a moment of this kind with Lea on our first meeting when, without my making mention of my mother, Lea opined that our relationship had not been good. I had never articulated that fact to myself but on her offering this insight, I knew absolutely that what she said was the truth. I saw in groups how Lea could ask a question or make a suggestion to the individual wanting help that could open up the scope of the issue at hand, throwing light upon it that could relieve the emotional oppression endured by that person. This was particularly true with respect to guilt and shame carried by people due to religious or cultural constraints. She had and imparted a healthy sense of humour about such issues.

As her practice grew, Lea gradually developed more skills. Meg remembered her speaking with surprise in 1964-5 about some of the things they were dealing with in the groups. Lea had opened up a depth of work that she hadn't really planned on and was sort of surprised that she could do it. Much of this work related to emotions deemed unacceptable or too frightening to be expressed, emotions such as rage and terror. When in a session or in a group a client revealed perhaps obliquely feelings of this kind, Lea would encourage her to go further into their expression, perhaps having other group members supporting her, all the while reassuring her that releasing the emotions freely was a healthy, not a negative endeavour. Lea was picking up skills like psychodrama from work being done by others in the field, using them in her own tool box.

In one of the Tuesday-Friday groups Lea had me relate an experience I had had with my father when I was about seven or eight. Its residue had been a sense of my being betrayed and physically abused by him. A man was assigned the role of my father: he acted as though he was in a loving mood with me, but then changed abruptly, intent upon punishing me because my mother had said that he must; the role-playing father pretended to hit me. With the encouragement of Lea and others surrounding me, I allowed myself to feel and express some of the anger that I felt about this incident.

This was more or less the landscape of Lea's developing practice until early 1964 when Gregory Baum, a theological professor at the Medieval Institute located at St Michael's College of the University of Toronto, contacted her. He had heard of her work through another student of his. Concerned about the mental health of one of his religious graduate students, Gregory came to meet Lea. They were intrigued with one another. Interestingly, though this would never have been a part of their discussion, both were of Jewish origin – Greg had been one of the children rescued from Germany just before the opening of WWII and sent to England for fostering and adoption. His graduate student began sessions with her. Other students of his, knowing of the referral, spoke with Greg about Lea, asking to be introduced to her. These were religious men and women from Canada, the United States, and Australia, who had come to study and receive advanced degrees at St Michael's with the intention of returning to their parishes or religious orders at completion. Many were interested in Lea's work because of their own needs, but also because by understanding what she was doing, they thought they might replicate some of it in their later roles as pastors or teachers.

In late March Lea started with them what became known as the Catholic group. A year later in June 1965, many of its members became the core of her first learning group, called the Hypnotherapy Group because of her extensive use of and teaching of hypnotherapy methods within the group. Other more mature, long-term clients like Grant, Gus, Meg, and Jack King, also were invited to join the learning group. Late in the previous year some members of the Catholic group had begun to move into recently purchased 59 Admiral Rd, and into 55 Admiral Rd purchased not long after. Already a number of these men and women had decided to leave religious life to continue their training and their own personal therapy, or were well on the road to this decision.

Adam C came to Toronto in 1965 to do a masters' degree at the Medieval Institute. He recalled, "The Catholic group was very impressive for me. I realized then that I was interested in this kind of thing. In the group people were speaking of things I had never experienced. And Lea was so unusual." Not long afterwards, Adam joined Lea's Monday morning group as well and moved into 55 Admiral.

"I got involved very quickly. It was exciting but also challenging because I was a very private person, and this was not private at all. Even though I had been part of a (religious) community. I had never been in one like this where people were together all the time, talking, staying up late and going out and doing things together. There was so much going on. There was so much energy."

Others came into the group via other avenues. Mike Quealey and Stan K at the Newman Centre heard of Lea because some of the students that they knew at St. Mike's were seeing her for therapy. Mike had helped one girl get out of a psychiatric unit because he could see that it wasn't doing her any good. He was counselling some fairly troubled kids but felt a lot of pressure because he knew that he was in over his head. When Mike heard that Greg Baum was involved with someone over on Admiral Road, he sent a couple of people to her and watched what happened. He liked what he saw. But it was still a long time before he got involved. He remembered,

"Much about Lea I liked in those early days. She would put pressure back on people in a very creative way, making them responsible no matter what degree of disturbance they had. In those days, she would say that the whole purpose of her work was to deliver people to themselves. She would say that therapy should be a short-term thing: you get as much out of it as you can and then you get right out there and live your life."

Mary Lou Dill (ML) was never a participant in the Catholic group though she was associated with it from her early days with Lea.

"I came to see Lea in July 1964 when she was at 477 Brunswick Ave. I started right away to see her for three sessions a week. A year or so later I went into a small group that met on Mondays. I did intensive work with her until I left the convent in August 1966. She was really at her best in those years. She had only the Brunswick and Howland houses and hadn't begun to expand so she wasn't exhausted and overwhelmed in the way that she became later. I moved into 59 Admiral Road around the time that the other religious people in the Catholic group were moving into 55 Admiral. I found being there very liberating as I had lived such a restricted life in my religious community. Suddenly I could do very much as I wished. I had a very good time there for the following year. It was fun. It was like being away at university but not having to go to classes. I answered the phone for Lea and let people in who were coming to see her. I was still doing therapy with her as well."

Therapy in 1966-67

In the summer of 1966 I approached Father Stan Kutz at the Newman Centre on the U of Toronto campus. I had just graduated from St Michael's College and had found a teaching job for the fall. But I was not happy. I had been in a religious community for four years before I came for my third year at St Mike's. I was not close to my family and the students with whom I studied were several years my junior. I was quite lonely. I was beginning to realize that I had difficulty making lasting relationships with either women or with men. I had been helped when I decided to leave the convent by a priest in Ottawa, so it seemed a natural step to talk again with a priest. I had gotten to know Stan and his co-worker Mike Quealey, a bit over the school year. I told Stan my situation and asked if he thought I needed to see a psychiatrist. He said no he didn't think so, but, he knew a woman who was doing group psychotherapy that he thought I would benefit from. The idea of entering into a group situation had great appeal for me. Stan gave me her phone number.

When I came to 59 Admiral the following week to meet with this Mrs. Smith, there was no Therafields. There was only Lea and her expanding practice. The advent of Greg Baum's students had moved Lea into wholly new dimensions not only in numbers but also in the kinds of therapies offered. The day that I met her, Lea was already ill and exhausted with over-work, but there was never a question of my not being accepted into her practice. During that period of rapid expansion, in great part through referrals made by Catholic group members, Lea took on everyone. By the time I came along, there were dozens of people wanting her help. Why she continued to accept new clients is an important question because her situation was clearly untenable. So many elements of Lea's own make-up come into answers of this question. She was moved by the people who came to her, seeing in them promise, seeing the troubles that blocked them from living fuller lives, and knowing that the therapy that she was evolving could be of help. There was literally little else available at the time in Toronto. She could not bring herself to refuse the people seeking her help. But, as became clear over time, it was also true that Lea would in certain mood states, take on more than she could handle. The entity known as Therafields came into being gradually over the next year or so as a result of ad hoc decisions and directions made as conditions arose.

Under the considerable weight of her practice that summer of 1966, Lea proposed that some of the members of her learning group begin to work with the new arrivals. In the month after I met her, Lea was beginning to make these assignments. When she spoke with me at the beginning of the month, she placed me in her Tuesday-Friday group and talked about working with me individually. Within a few weeks, however, she assigned me to one of the newly-minted therapists, Marty P. I was to continue in her Tuesday-Friday group and to have individual sessions with Marty. In this arrangement, I would have a therapist with enough time to see me twice a week, as well as the benefit of Lea's expertise in the group. At the same time seeing me in her group would allow Lea an on-going sense of my issues so that she could supervise Marty's work in the learning/seminar group. This solution to the impossible demand on Lea's time and energy by so many new clients had its up and its down sides. The most obvious benefit was that most of us who came to Lea then and in subsequent years could not otherwise have been admitted into her practice. The arrangement also gave to her fledgling learners actual clients with whom to begin an apprenticeship in her art. It gave Lea breathing space and made possible her decision the following year to address her own serious health issues.

The downside has at least two components, problems that recurred as each succeeding "generation" of new therapists took on clients of their own. Firstly, the people who began to work varied greatly in the depth of their own personal troubles and therapies. Some had had few sessions of their own and had done whatever work did occur in the group setting. It's pretty much a truism that you cannot take people where you have not gone yourself. If I have blind spots, areas of denial, or split off components, I will be unable to detect them in you, let alone be able to assist you in recognizing and resolving them. The second difficulty arose from the very power of Lea's personality and work in her groups. At the core of psycho-therapeutic practice is the resolution of what is called 'transference.' At every level of learning we 'transfer' one piece of knowledge to ever-broadening contexts. For example, we learn the concept 'tree' by an early identification of a particular tree by a care-giver. We transfer that piece of knowledge then to all those entities that present similar characteristics. We do not have to learn over and over again with every specimen, the meaning of 'tree.'

On neurological and emotional levels the process is similar. If our early home is safe and loving, we learn at a nervous system level to trust and relax with others. If there are external threats like war, the tensions and fears they engender in our parents are communicated to us in ways that thwart our own capacity to be at ease in the world. More generally, the atmosphere of the home in which we develop as little creatures, impacts the whole of how we later live in and deal with the world. We are like the little fish in a fish bowl, breathing in whatever the watery atmosphere provides. Those elements affect and shape major components of our emotional and physical capacities to deal with our lives.

The reality of these effects can be seen everywhere. Growing up with an authoritative father, a young adult might bow to the authority of other figures like teachers or bosses to such a degree that it precludes a developing sense of himself. Or, he might rebel against authority figures in ways that sap his capacity to make decisions that are good for him. Whatever stresses we grow up with that are unresolved, we will continue to live with in some fashion, not necessarily conscious to us, but always at work within the landscape of our lives. Inevitably we will find conditions or individuals upon which or whom we will project our unresolved painful, frightened, or needy experiences and emotions. In a therapeutic context, the therapist can become the template upon which the client projects longings as well as fears. Handled with understanding and compassion, the client can, over time, connect with, understand, and ventilate the pain, the rage, the terror of early experiences, and thus be liberated to a deeper self knowledge and emotional maturity with which to deal with life, work, and love.

In the dispensation of therapeutic work established in 1966, many of us centred our transference on Lea rather than with our own individual worker. Lea was clearly the parent; the other therapist was more like an older sibling, albeit, in the main a kind and well-meaning one. With some clients, the transference was split. In a situation like this, resolution of the all-important transference material is next to impossible. At the core of many of my own troubles, for example, lay profound fear of my mother, engendered doubtless in the early years of her marriage and motherhood. Alone during the working week with three children under the age of six, her own limited resources were insufficient to allow her an easy relationship with her children. In frustration she would yell, hit, and treat brusquely whomever might be taxing her strength. I feared her but also yearned for her love and acceptance.

On first meeting Lea I was impressed by her kindliness, intelligence, and perception. In my early days in her group Lea became for me the mother I had longed for, the one who could love, accept, and encourage me. Within a year, however, as I became less defended from my feelings of fear, being around Lea became more complicated and uncomfortable. Much of what was happening to me lay under my own conscious radar. I didn't talk with Marty or in a group about my feelings. By the time they had become more consciously focused on Lea, she was not in any workable context available to me. Now, I would know what to do: I would ask for a context in which to talk with her. Then, I simply did what I had done in the past in similar circumstances: I avoided her. If I had been Lea's client in those early days, I am certain that she would have been aware of my ambivalence toward her and would have brought it to the surface where I could express the fear and rage that I had held for years (and continued to hold for years after this period), as well as the longings that I had. This is the working through of the transference. None of us, Lea included, understood the dynamics created by the arrangement of our essentially having two different therapists.

At this point Lea had three different kinds of groups: "standard" groups; house groups; and learning groups. The standard groups met twice weekly. They were the second level of introduction to therapy – the first being individual sessions (usually twice a week) with a therapist. Individual sessions continued with the addition of the group work. House groups were constellations of people living in a particular house with one another. In 1966-7 the members of each house group met with Lea weekly. Learning groups were composed of individuals who had shown an interest in and a capacity for becoming therapists themselves. These groups would meet with Lea at least once a week. In practice there was a lot of overlap among the groups. For example, by the early fall of 1966 I was seeing Marty twice a week, was in Lea's Tuesday-Friday group meeting in the late afternoon on both of those days, and, was in a house group on the third floor of the apartment building at 32 Admiral Rd, meeting with Lea on Sunday mornings. A person in a learning group would also be living in a house group and would be embedded in one of Lea's standard groups as well as a learner. Clearly, the hours of therapy could tally to six a week, even more if are factored in the time in the house groups themselves of people talking with one another about their troubles.

In May 1967 Lea spoke in my standard Tuesday-Friday group about a weekend of therapy work she had just spent with her Hypnotherapy learning group at the Anglican Centre in Aurora. The weekend had been productive; many people experienced important breakthroughs in their therapy. Our group asked if we could do the same thing. Soon afterwards, we were off to the Cedar Glen United Church retreat house in Bolton for a weekend. It was explained to the administration of the centre that we were an experimental acting group – to alleviate any concerns they might have about raised voices or less than polite language. We drove up Friday evening and met as a group for a few hours. In the morning after breakfast we continued. There was an early afternoon break and a late afternoon session. In the evening we listened to music and talked and relaxed. On Sunday we continued until after lunch when we returned to the city.

I found the "marathon," as these long gatherings came to be called, intense and interesting. Lea conducted it as she did all her regular groups. We (roughly 25 people) would gather in a large room. Someone, or sometimes several people, would announce that they wanted to talk about some concern of theirs. One would launch into his or her issue and Lea would work with it – sometimes referring to experiences in the person's past that she knew of that related to the difficulty raised. Some of the embedded learners would at times speak too, relating ways that they experienced or dealt with similar problems. If someone told a dream Lea would often ask if anyone would like to interpret it. The sessions were collaborative and on-going learning situations. Very often the difficulties spoken of by one person would relate to the experience or problems of others and speaking of them would generate other dimensions or directions.

In groups Lea always encouraged people to read authors whom she had found helpful in formulating her own understanding of human behaviour and emotion. In my standard group, for example, she would often refer to a Catherine Cookson book that she had just finished reading. Cookson was a contemporary of Lea's, born in 1906 and living until 1998. She began writing about 1950 and published over 100 novels. Her stories are set in an England familiar to Lea; they showcase romance, class struggle, 'wickedness,' and often, the triumph of good. The stories are quite readable. They would make a point that Lea was perhaps stressing in her work with someone in the group. This type of reference was quite in tune with Lea's method of working in the group at that time. She rarely, if ever, used academic or psychological terms, and she did not give analyses according to any school or theory. Rather she would invite a person to speak about their trouble, asking for an example to illuminate the way that the problem was typically acted out. From this example she could often reach an understanding of the roots of the trouble. She made use of her knowledge of the person, her experience with and understanding of relationships, and her intuition. Simply being in the group was a learning experience as one observed her moving quite organically from the confusions of the speaker to a more clearly enunciated understanding of what was happening. The results could be quite moving as the work sometimes opened the speaker to another level of feeling and awareness of him or her self.

Lea would speak of Freud, though certainly not in terms of any theory of his. She encouraged the reading of his works, especially the *New Introductory Lectures,* a most readable account of the basic workings of the unconscious mind. Another book that she recommended was *Man's Presumptuous Brain: An Evolutionary Interpretation of Psychosomatic Disease* by A.T.W. Simeons, MD. I had had courses in human anatomy and physiology, so the base information of this book was not difficult for me. Simeons's interpretation made enormous sense, especially in conceptualizing the power of body-work which some of us took on after the Character Analysis Group was founded in 1968. We read also Robert Lindner's set of case studies in the *Fifty Minute Hour.* They were all interesting. Lea's stress was on learning about psychodynamic psychotherapy, on learning to think broadly, and to challenge conformity in oneself. In 1967, a new approach became available with Alexander Lowen's book, *The Betrayal of the Body*. I recognized immediately the value of his work, sensing that it advanced a practical path forward to emotional and physical health.

A question about people marrying and having children surfaced briefly during the Cedar Glen marathon. This issue loomed large for Lea and especially for the young women of Therafields years later in the mid-1970s. Lea may have been speaking to or commenting on something said by one of the participants during one session. She looked thoughtful, saying that contrary to popular wisdom, not everyone would be wise to marry and have children. I felt threatened in some fashion by this pronouncement and said almost petulantly, "Well, I certainly intend to marry and have children." Lea looked and me and said quietly, "Yes, you will marry."

During our time at Cedar Glen, Lea and others spoke about how great it would be to have a place of our own where all the various groups could regularly meet for more extended periods. Dan McDonald, Lea and a few others went to look at a farm that was for sale near Mono Mills – the farm that was to become known as Therafields. Very soon afterwards money was raised primarily from the Hypnotherapy Group to purchase the farm. It cost around $60,000. We got possession of it in late August, 1967.

The Marathon at Bigwin Resort

Earlier in 1967 the pressure of Lea's schedule and her declining health meant fewer sessions and less individual work with her regular clients and her learning therapists. Yet many clearly needed a forum to address and work with problems that were close to the surface. Lea proposed in June a two-week "holiday"/marathon at Bigwin Island, a resort north of Toronto, as a possible solution. The large group of the learners as well as others considered too fragile to be left alone in Toronto without Lea or their own therapist, headed for the resort at Bigwin. There, she used all the tools of her craft: relaxation, dream analysis, psychodrama, and increasingly, physical (i.e., physically interactive) work. Disturbed material poured forth from participant after participant. By the end of the first week, however, the context felt less safe and more chaotic as the sheer number of people close to their own raw emotional states increased and the resulting number of those able to ground and support them decreased. Connecting with scary, disturbing feelings and memories within a therapy context is only one, albeit, important moment on a path to resolution. A great deal of "mop-up" work must follow. The client must feel in a sense "contained" within a context of quite substantial support in order to explore, connect with, and articulate formerly repressed feelings and the ways they have been active in his or her daily life. Lea came to Bigwin hoping to deal with and resolve a back-load of therapeutic material with her hypnotherapy learners, but in the event even more was released.

This "holiday" and marathon marked an important watershed experience for the whole community. A more active form of therapy was begun there – a deliberate provoking of material combined with the kinds of psychodrama that Lea already used to a certain extent. The work stirred enormous depths of fairly primitive, formerly repressed material for many of the participants, including for Lea herself. It was too much too fast. Methods and understandings gained from that period continued to be implemented with other groups, but for some of the actual Bigwin participants their breakthroughs had no substantial follow-up. There simply were not the resources to handle the work that it had engendered and Lea herself was overwhelmed.

At the core of any person's troubles lie primitive fears beyond his or her conscious reach but which are acted out in some form in daily life as well as in the structure and functioning of his or her body. Over the years of her own apprenticeship as a therapist in Toronto, Lea gradually developed confidence in working with deeper levels in her clients as they were revealed. Group work, especially in a marathon setting, allowed an intense but safe context within which terrors and their resulting rages could be flushed to the surface. Lea and the other group members could surround and support an individual through this experience both within the group and later, outside of it. Supporters would supply the sense of calm understanding, acceptance, and love necessary to an integration and thus resolution of the formerly repressed material.

The process worked so long as Lea herself was well and truly grounded and if she had enough solid assistance in her groups. However, even as marathon work was developing in 1967-8, those conditions were failing. If I have repressed feelings and experiences, witnessing or being involved with another's expression of these can not only push my own emotions to the surface, but it can give me tacit permission to express them. This is the power of the group experience. But it is also its danger. If too many in the group are overwhelmed with their troubles and there are not enough supporters to assist them, not enough energy in the group or in the therapist to facilitate this intensely demanding work, the experience can replicate the terror and chaos of the individual's original situation and further repression ensue. Lea was not unaware of these possibilities. She would speak of the scriptural parable about the man from whom a devil was cast out who was later invaded by a host of seven more. She warned about experimental sensitivity groups then in vogue in California and other locales -- T-groups, for example, because of damage done when people were indiscriminately opened to their deepest troubles and then basically abandoned without follow-up.

People who had previously done substantial work with Lea date that period as the end of their personal therapy with her. The farm had already been purchased and work would soon begin to turn it into a centre for marathons. Lea's group and individual schedule were impossibly over-taxed. The nascent community now demanded not only Lea's time and energy but as well that of many of the Bigwin participants. The learning group became more of a seminar and less a place in which personal work could happen. But the real centre of change that made the continuation of deep and consistent work for Lea's clients/learners was within Lea herself. Even before the farm and the Therafields name and institution came into being, the first seeds of its demise had been sown.

Lea had presented herself as a woman from a generous, supportive and creative family, who had in her turn produced a similar family of her own. Stories told by her in groups drawn from her own life and those of her children would highlight those qualities. But this picture did not capture the full range of her experiences. In fact, Lea was living in denial about her family of origin and about her children. Her failure to come to terms with this would have long term consequences for her practice, and for Therafields in general. Meg K, who was close to her in those years and for the next decade said,

> "When Lea talked about her family it didn't make sense. She would speak of these wonderful people on her mother's side, every member of whom was accomplished and terrific in every way, yet they didn't seem to be around. Later, details would be filled in but what she said seemed rather abstract. When I saw her with her own children there wasn't the kind of cohesive, warm emotional base one would expect in a family that was portrayed as so wonderful."

Material from her own early life which Lea had been able to rise above earlier surged to the surface with the combined pressures of failing health and energy and the depth of the work done at Bigwin. Her own early terrors and her profound sense of abandonment by her nanny and father surfaced but were never worked with in a way that could allow for resolution. The failure of Lea's defensive structures over the period 1967-8 presaged not a deeper level of self-awareness but rather new structures of defence as well as new ways of life and a truly altered relationship with what had formerly been her therapy practice. It is during that period that the farm was purchased and developed. New forms of organization were clearly necessary.

The Farm

On the first weekend of September 1967, when we came into possession of the farm, a group of men went there to demolish the interior of a large tool shed close to the farmhouse, preparatory to making it into a group room. At Lea's groups during the week that followed, she spoke of the work they had done. Keen to be a part of the process, many of us volunteered to work there on the up-coming weekend. That Saturday, a veritable horde swarmed up to tackle the barn. I was among them. Our main task was to scrape a century of dirt from the beams of the former cattle and horse pens in the lower barn. Given chairs or ladders and long, stiff brushes, we stood for hours in the large, rather dank space pulling down unspeakable grunge onto our covered heads. The atmosphere was amazingly excited and fun. That lower section of the barn was slated to become two dormitories – men's and women's, a large dining room, a kitchen and two washrooms. Some from the group of workers bought groceries and cooked lunch and supper at the farmhouse.

At noon, we sat on its stoop and lawn and ate our meal together. After supper that evening we sat about singing and visiting as one worker played his guitar. Some of us stayed overnight – sleeping in improvised bedrolls on the floor in the farmhouse – keen to be available for more work on Sunday. Others returned to the city and came back again the next day. So began the pattern for the fall: people who were not working at regular jobs would come up during the week; others would come after work for the evening; on the weekends larger numbers would come. We were young and healthy and very into the whole project of making a place for ourselves.

People like my house-mate, Don, who was a carpenter, John N (a pseudonym), an architect, and others were especially important in the organization and oversight of the work. Lea spent a lot of time up there that fall, living in the farmhouse. She applied her energies to overseeing the shape and direction of the building. She chose materials for pillows and bedspreads for the dormitory bunk beds and generally was involved with the women's side of the project. She was also in constant touch with the men about the scope and planning of the facilities. People in her standard, house and learning groups were kept up to date on the progress of the work and were inspired by her enthusiasm and by the whole spirit of the project to volunteer their time. It was exciting. Being there every weekend, we got to work with and to know other people across the range of the community. At some point that fall Lea came up with the idea of calling the farm "Therafields." – i.e., therapy plus the fields of the farm. Before Christmas, the farm was ready for marathons though construction and renovation continued in various phases for years: up-grading the kitchen and bathrooms; developing a new and elaborate entrance way; building smaller group rooms and bedrooms and developing a theatre/ communal space in the upper loft; building "Striders" – a large Quonset hut workshop (its name taken from Tolkien's *Fellowship of the Ring*, a root cellar, a greenhouse; and, expanding the farmhouse to include better facilities and more bedrooms, primarily for the "farm group," the people who began to live and work there on a permanent basis.

The farm house

The barn

An Early Warning Sign

Into the midst of all of this excitement and development came an incident which, in retrospect, highlights an approach that Lea was to take over the years with respect to families with children. The story began a year earlier but only got traction in the summer and fall of 1967. When I moved into the third floor of 32 Admiral Rd in October, 1966, a young couple, whom I will call Margaret and Jack, was already living there. Margaret was expecting a child. Because Margaret was in the Tuesday-Friday group, as was I, it was clear to me that she was suffering from profound depression. Around the time that the baby, Lisa, was born late in the year, the couple moved down to a basement apartment in the building. This may have been conceived as a suitable domestic situation for them, but in fact the increased isolation this arrangement brought was not salutary. Margaret's depression did not lift with the birth of the child. It very likely became worse. In the atmosphere of the third floor group with several mature, goodhearted people, the couple could have been given support to see them through this difficult period. Concern arose about the couples' ability to care for the baby properly, but the idea of moving them back into a supportive milieu was never broached. Josie, Lea's 21-year old daughter, lived in another basement apartment with her husband and their baby, Matthew. Dropping in for a visit with Jack and Margret, Josie detected an ear infection in the baby that had not been attended to. On the strength of this she confided to her mother that the baby might be in danger.

A few years earlier, Lea had arranged for the removal of another child from his parents' home. She was convinced that she had saved his life. In groups, Lea would speak of that experience, congratulating herself on stepping in. Over the years, however, that "saved" boy lived in diverse family constellations, during his teen years staying at the farm more or less a ward of Therafields. He did not prosper. Still, Lea's idea that her intervention had been "life-saving," no doubt influenced her thinking in the second child's case. In subsequent years as Lea's judgment and balance became precarious. Interference in the lives of families was repeated with bad outcomes. Lea began to lose the elasticity of mind and approach that had characterized her earlier work.

The proposed arrangement resembled that made, for example, by children's aid societies. There is a problem. Take the child out of the home. But the cure was often worse for the child than the problem. The focus of Lea's concern seems to have been "an inadequacy of maternal care." She talked about Margaret's situation in another of her groups. An older couple was approached or volunteered to take the child for a time to give Margaret a chance to "work through" her problems. So it played out. Just a month or so old, the baby Lisa was taken off to Peterborough to live with that family. By the late summer of 1967 the baby was about 10 months old. The foster mother was voicing concern to Lea that Lisa had clearly bonded with her. Either she and her husband should adopt her, or she should be returned to her mother. With the farm available, Lea decided to take Margaret, the baby, and a group of support people up to the farmhouse for a week or so to help Margaret get accustomed to Lisa in a safe situation. Because I had that week free and had had some involvement with the baby in the brief time she was at 32 Admiral Rd, I asked if I could go along to help.

Glenda M drove up with me. Lea, Margaret, Lisa, Adam, Mary Lou (ML), and Barrie (bp Nichol) were all part of the contingent – possibly Meg as well. Glenda and I did a lot of the domestic work – buying groceries and cooking and keeping the place clean. ML was more involved with Lisa's care. Margaret remained very depressed and was not as responsive to Lisa as had been hoped. The period of separation from her baby had not in fact given her an opportunity to 'work through' her problems. The psychiatric treatment for depression in that period was electric shock applied to the brain. It was primitive. Its effects were sometimes helpful but it could also cause serious loss of memory. Lea had little of help to say about depression. She herself had had severe bouts of it. She would say, in fact, that no one had suffered more from depression than had she. She would ride them out, finding solace in being with friends. I have no doubt that Margaret's depression, whatever its causes, could only have been exacerbated by the loss of her child and the complications of shame and guilt that would have been attendant.

Gradually ML became the primary care giver. I sat in on some, though not all, of the groups formed to work with Margaret. In one I was startled to hear Lea telling Margaret in strident tones that she was a paranoid schizophrenic. This appeared to me a rather extravagant diagnosis. I had been exposed to schizophrenic patients during my three-month psychiatric affiliation while in nurses' training and Margaret showed none of the features that I had observed. It didn't occur to me to contradict Lea's assertion. I was too far gone in the thrall of her personality and authority. Only much later in retrospect, did I put together what I had found so shocking and even abusive about the way that she spoke to Margaret. Her tone was not at all kindly; rather it was an accusation hurled at the young woman, as if by baldly stating a disagreeable fact she could force her out of it. Perhaps she hoped to provoke Margaret's rage that lay not far from the surface.

After a week, I went back to the city to my job but most of the others stayed on for months, forming the nucleus of the first farm group. ML was signalled by Lea to take over Lisa's care and she responded to the challenge. She and Stan K had been seeing each other and now a little family was formed with them and the baby. Margaret remained for a time mainly engaged in on-going work about the farm. Throughout, Lisa's father Jack, was not considered or brought on board. Though not happy about the arrangements, he went along with the prevailing group wisdom that Lea knew best and that Lisa primarily needed a responsive woman for her care.

There was public fall-out from the situation. Newspapers picked up the outrage expressed by Margaret's parents who lived in a community up north, that their grandchild had been given away. Reporters were eager to hear about the group and about what had happened. Several newspaper articles were printed, leading to a brief notoriety that Lea and others found painful and threatening. I remember the concerned tones in which this publicity was discussed and how eager Lea and others were to avoid any repetition of it. There wasn't, however, any questioning of the actual events or of Lea's judgment. Two very young people had allowed their baby to be taken away on slim evidence of trouble. When the child had bonded with the second set of parents, she was again uprooted and allocated to a third. This sequence of events had long-term damaging effects for all concerned.

A New Administration

By the late fall of 1967 what had been Lea's private practice had evolved into a conglomerate of several hundred people, many of whom lived in house groups and were in learning groups. The demands of the community – with its various houses and now the farm -- far outweighed Lea's capacity to administer. She had begun plans to go to a clinic in North Carolina early in the new year to deal with her diagnosed type-2 diabetes and needed to establish lines of command before leaving. Leadership at the farm had evolved that fall as individuals with time, energy and skills came forward and took charge. Adam was there quite a bit as part of the on-going project with Lisa at the farm house. As ML was involved in the project, Stan also was present much of the time. That academic year he was teaching at St Mike's College and living in the city, but he spent every moment not in class at the farm. He took charge of the construction work, ordered supplies and worked with other volunteers fashioning the group room and the communal living areas.

There was another site in which leadership was needed: Lea's groups, including the seminar/learning group when Lea was not present. If she could not attend a group or would be late, Lea would ask Rob, Barrie or sometimes Josie to sit in on the group to let her know what had happened. This became 'taking the therapist's chair,' an importantly symbolic act. From being an observer to "taking" the group was a slippery slope in these circumstances. By late 1967 it was common practice that Rob and Barrie would chair the seminar meetings in Lea's absence. They would bring concerns of hers to the meetings and in turn would relay to her the substance of the discussions. There was no dissension in the group about this arrangement.

At a seminar meeting that she called in December 1967 at the farm, Lea wanted to talk about how it would be cared for while she was away. Lea used a "soft" approach to get what she wanted: "Let's talk about this. What do you think? What should we do?" etc. Stan was proposed as the obvious choice to continue the leadership role that he had assumed at the farm. No, Lea said. Stan has made some bad decisions -- he had once ordered too much concrete; he wasn't a good choice. Well, how about (another person)? No, he's not mature enough. What about so-and-so? No, I don't feel good about him. Each proposal was rejected. Clearly, she had someone in mind. At last Rob was suggested. Lea clapped her hands together with delight. Of course, what a brilliant idea. She immediately coupled Barrie with Rob and spoke of how well they would work together.

Rob was then 19 years old; he had not completed high school, had never held a job, and had no experience of management, but, he was his mom's right-hand boy. He was her closest child, her consolation in the years of developing estrangement with Harry, and the child who had not rebelled against her as had Malcolm and Josie. Rob always experienced himself as the arbiter in the family, the go-between for his parents, his siblings, and, between his parents and his siblings. He had gotten along at school despite bullying incidents, by becoming a clown. He had a quick wit and could be funny, and he used these skills to defuse situations of tension. Lea trusted him because he was always there, always faithful to her, always hers. Doing some high school courses at home, he had had the leisure to become involved with the learning group, doing "therapy" in the group itself with his mother, and sharing a room in the family suite on the ground floor of 59 Admiral with Barrie, Lea's other "son" of trust and closeness.

Barrie is, in literary and artistic circles, known as bpNicholl, a distinguished Canadian poet, winner of a Governor General's award. In 1967, the period of which I am writing, he was 23 years old. He was profoundly in debt to Lea. Like Rob he was his mother's last child. He had left home but his therapy with Lea had shifted his feelings for his mother to her. Lea encouraged him in his poetry and in his personal development, but she kept him close. He was as solidly hers as was Rob. For the next decade, this special arrangement endured. "The boys" as Lea referred to them in her writings, were tuned into her concerns and needs and they followed her directions and supported her unflinchingly.

Rob Henley-Smith in the 1970s.

Barrie (bpNichol) in the mid-1960s

Lea and what was formerly her therapy practice were at an important crossroads in late 1967. I think that even before she went to North Carolina, Lea intuited that she would never return to her practice as it had been. It was no longer possible for her either physically or emotionally. Up until the purchase of the farm, the properties used by her clients were her own. Now something new was happening. The number of people swelling the ranks was bringing financial resources that could open other possibilities. Lea was a fighter and a survivor. She had come alone from Wales to find her way in London with little backing; she had survived the Great Depression, World War II, and the insecurities of the family's early years in Canada. She started with little and had developed a small real estate portfolio of her own. Moreover, her therapy practice of inauspicious beginnings had grown into a "community" of several hundred people. Lea was not about to surrender the centrality of her own position, especially during this time of personal vulnerability. Lea distributed her clients and her groups to the learners but to Rob and Barrie she bequeathed the role of practical administration, subject always to her approval. Thus, Lea put her stamp upon the future. Rob and Barrie would be her executives; she would be governor.

In my interviews, I did not come across much strong feeling about Lea's placing "the boys" in charge in 1967. Dan MacDonald, Mike Quealey and other members of the seminar were aware of the manner in which Lea had managed to push through her intentions. She had orchestrated Rob and Barrie's appointment without the overt show of power she exhibited the following year after her return. Most simply accepted the decision without a struggle. One remembers that,

> "When Lea went away to North Carolina she left Rob and Barrie in charge which was absolutely crazy. She would bring up that kind of idea: 'Wouldn't it be great for them to lead things? They work so well together.' Then it would happen. There wasn't much talk about it, but it wasn't a surprise. By then they were chairing the group when she wasn't there. But they were 'puer' in the Jungian sense -- the boys. We allowed them to take over by not intervening. The number of core people in the group who

had come out of religious life aided this giving over. What was best in religious life was camaraderie and the feeling of connection with one another. We were not used to reflecting deeply on economic aspects".

In religious life another important value was obedience, even in spirit, to the directions of one's superior. Lea had established herself and had been established by this group as the one who would set directions in all important areas. She wanted to remain in control of the evolving landscape of Therafields and knew that her best hope was to place the young men at the helm in her absence.

Many of the former theology students, by then seminar members, were mature people with a wide variety of experiences. Lea clearly did not intend that any one of them or any small group of them would administer Therafields. Already she was aware that some had opinions that were not entirely aligned with her own. She feared their power and circumvented any growth of it by ensuring that the administration of Therafields remained in her own pocket – i.e., with Rob and Barrie. I doubt that Lea saw clearly that she was in a power struggle with the seminar at the time. She probably would have been horrified to have these facts spelled out so baldly. And few would have realized that that was what was happening. But there were some who knew that Lea resisted abler administrators and did not openly challenge her choice. There was no collectively separate voice within the seminar group. It did not see itself as an entity distinct from Lea. Each person had in different ways a relationship with her that was based on respect, gratitude for her teaching and therapy, and, to greater or lesser degrees, on positive and/or negative transference. When she returned from North Carolina, however, a newly restored Lea more directly asserted control in ways that ultimately interrupted the harmony of the seminar. All of these factors made the development of contrary opinion difficult and slow, even dangerous to any individual who attempted to voice it openly.

Gradually over this period Lea was developing a cadre of helpers and supporters. All had been clients of hers and most were now in learning groups. Many had received little individual therapy. People who had worked with Lea before the emergence of Therafields had had a much longer period of individual and group therapy and hence a stronger personal foundation. But after 1965, Lea was simply too busy to dedicate as much individual time to clients. Sometimes they would see her for a few sessions, but mainly did their work in the group settings. As they moved into learning groups and lived in proximity to Lea in the 55-59 Admiral Rd complex, their relationships with her changed and their positions as clients became blurred. Each became client, colleague, and assistant. Essentially the possibilities of any substantial therapeutic work ended. Glenda and Meg were her masseuses; Stella became her secretary and housekeeper; others like Adam and Mike Quealey became her assistants in group work. As the core of therapeutic resolution remains the working through of transference, the positive and negative emotional residues of childhood experience, all of those "elevated" into Lea's inner circle or 'family' were stymied in his or her own progress. Their special positions made each vulnerable to giving over themselves to the needs, ideas, and directions of Lea. They simply did not, could not, stand up to her, particularly in any public forum. Like Rob and Barrie, they had become hers.

People not taken into the inner 'court' were more able to challenge Lea about issues that she promoted. But each would be 'worked with,' not just by Lea but by her assistants and others who wanted to be seen as on her team. The dissident would be reduced, often humiliated publicly. I experienced this treatment in 1975 after I returned from a vacation in Florida. Josie, Lea's daughter, had become my therapist a couple of months earlier. She was in Florida at the same time as I. I felt uncomfortable about the relationship between us. While we were there space in the house was limited and Josie arranged for me to share a room with her and her young son. Over several days she drew me into a place of 'friendship' with her, talking with me at some length about her own current sexual life. There was an overtone in all of our interactions that I found odd and disquieting.

I came back to Toronto just before the beginning of a weekend marathon at the farm for the Character Analysis group, of which I was a part. Lea was away so Rob and Barrie were the facilitators. The previous summer on a marathon I had spoken about some dysfunctional elements in my relationship with another woman who had been my therapist for four years. My experiences were listened to and validated. The woman about whom I had spoken was not by any means a part of the inner circle/family of Lea. But when I began to talk about my experience with Josie in Florida,

Rob and Barrie both reacted as if in shock. How could I say such things about Josie? They knew her to be a fine therapist, one who would never subject a client to the conditions of which I was speaking. It was all my own problem, likely unexpressed feelings that I had toward her. I was thwarted from what I knew to be true and humiliated in the company of my peers.

Lea did not understand or did not allow herself to understand the effect that her constantly shifting boundaries had on her clients and on her familiars. By then she was overwhelmed internally as well as externally and was unable to recognize or to acknowledge the directions she was following.

In fact, I don't believe that Lea ever fully understood or adopted the kind of boundaries between therapist and client that most of us now would see as essential to good working relations. Even in her early work as a therapist, Lea would trade services with a client. For example, Olive, a woman who later lived at 59 Admiral with her husband, did housecleaning for Lea in exchange for sessions. Members of Lea's early groups moved into houses with her, living somewhat separately from the family, but drawn into complex relationships with her and her family. Lea did this for many reasons, some of which were kindly in their intent, but which served other purposes as well. They allowed her to purchase large and beautiful homes for which she had a trained eye. Her clients, people well connected with her, paid the expenses through their rents and took good care of the houses as they appreciated in value. Lea was a smart businesswoman; buying and selling of properties in the 1950s and 1960s made her a wealthy woman. With her younger son Rob living at home, and later as Josie and Malcolm returned, she used the houses and the people living there as assistants in her project of giving to her children what she hoped would solve the emotional dilemmas of her family. Drawing clients into roles in her personal and professional life in the late 1960s was just a further development of the blurring of boundaries that had existed from the beginning to some degree.

Meeting Visvaldis

One of the most startling examples of poor boundaries developed over the year of 1967-8 as Lea became involved with Visvaldis Upaniks. Visvaldis' wife, whom Lea refers to as Mildred in her writings (I will continue this usage), was in Lea's Monday-Thursday group. In early 1967, Mildred spoke in the group of her fears for her husband, then recovering in hospital from an attempted suicide. He was an architect, an alcoholic, and an inveterate womanizer. Mildred had cared for and worried about him for years. Lea loved a challenge and he sounded interesting. In fact, she had already heard of him in the context of an affair that he had had with the former girl friend of one of her learners. Lea volunteered to visit him in the hospital. At their meeting, she promised to see him daily if he could get himself discharged. We hear now from researchers that it can take about 1/5th of a second to "fall in love." I doubt that it took much longer than that for Lea and Visvaldis to recognize something powerful in each other that they wanted and were looking for. Within a couple of weeks Lea was confessing her feelings for her new client to Mike Quealey and asking for "advice," i.e., the blanket approval and support that in that stage of his relationship with her, Mike was giving.

Any idea that Lea was strictly an asexual, maternal figure prior to her physical work in North Carolina a year later is belied by the awareness that many had of her restlessness in her marriage. She clearly wanted an equal partner, a consort with whom she could find satisfaction in the many levels of her life at that period. Her interest in some of the men with whom she worked went beyond the strictly therapeutic. Joe Daugherty, Tom McNeil, and Mike Quealey were some of those to whom she was drawn. One of the men close to the pre-1967 scene confessed that he felt relief when Lea and Visvaldis got together.

An important feature of Lea's story in Canada is that she had no personal life outside her immediate family. All her energy initially went into keeping the family afloat, and then into developing her practice. She had no external context in which to talk about her frustrations and troubles or to get objective feedback about her decisions. She had no "community" of her own in which to develop personal friendships, meet potential lovers, or get supervision for the work she was doing. Her entire context was her practice and it was from this world that she chose "friends," and confidants. And it was within this context that consciously or not she was seeking a mate. For Lea to develop a sexual relationship with one of the men with whom she had worked would have raised ethical questions to be sure. Those would not have been as serious, however, as the ones raised by her involvement with Visvaldis. He was in a quite broken state when she met him. Within a couple of weeks, she was confessing her attraction and desire to Mike. She did not pass Visvaldis on to another therapist, however, but continued to "work" with him, intensifying the bond between them and the need that they had for each other.

The other, more serious ethical lapse in this situation relates to "Mildred," Visvaldis' long-suffering wife. Mildred continued in Lea's group and to work with the Hypnoanalysis therapist to whom she had been assigned. As a member of Lea's group, was she also Lea's client? I would say that she was. She had looked in trust to Lea for help in her marriage. Instead, her husband had been swept up in an intensely emotional, later sexual involvement with the therapist to whom she had turned. That this was happening was clear to many of the members of the learning group. Weekly they listened to the tapes from the Monday-Thursday group as a learning mechanism and they were present at the marathon called in May at Prudhomme's motel for that group, when Visvaldis appeared as a "guest." They had heard Mildred's plea for help and now met the man himself. Some of these people may have been monks and nuns but they were not fools. One said to me,

> "What was so startling was that Lea showed up with Visvaldis at the Prudhomme marathon. It was so imprudent, unethical and unprofessional -- especially with his wife there in the group. There was real madness

to it. Part of it was her desire to have a man to help her. It was her insecurity, a compulsive, ungrounded element."

In 1976 Lea wrote about an early morning phone call from Visvaldis in Dec 1968. It was published a year later in the Therafields 15th anniversary booklet. The language used in what appears to be a monologue by Visvaldis is classically Lea's own, especially seen in the works she was writing at that time, though certainly some of the sentiments were Visvaldis' own. In it Visvaldis says, "I spoke to Mildred a while ago about all this (his vision and ideas for Therafields) but she frowned on everything. Instantly I felt castrated and found my ideas scattering. But now as I talk to you I can feel them all being drawn back together again." Mildred had referred to his ideas as "harebrained." She had become the foil to Lea, who represented an ideal woman and partner. During that period, Lea developed her typology of the paranoid/paranee. Her husband, Harry, and Visvaldis' wife, Mildred, became the archetypal paranoids from whom she and Visvaldis needed to separate in order to live healthy and productive lives. Lea wanted what she wanted, and she took what she wanted though she could not simply say so. Instead she had to elude even her own conscience by developing a theory to explain and justify actions which today would prompt the loss of her licence in any professional association.

Return From North Carolina

Lea in the early 1970s

In January 1968 Lea and Harry went to a clinic at Duke University in North Carolina that specialized in Type-2 diabetes. She was placed on a special diet and a regime of exercise to curb her out-of-control blood sugar level. When she returned the changes in her were strikingly visible. Not only had Lea lost a fair amount of weight, but she emerged as a person concerned with her appearance. Gone were the formless dresses and untidy hair. She presented an entirely new image with stylish clothing, high heels, make-up and well-coiffed hair-dos. But the changes went much deeper than the surface. Lea believed that she had been close to death in her illness and that many of her health problems derived from the constant giving of herself to her therapy practice and her family. She returned to Toronto determined to carve out a different life for herself. This did not mean, however, relinquishing her pivotal role in Therafields. Instead, it meant giving up not just much of the regular practice of therapy that she had been involved with for over a decade, but importantly, the approaches that she had taken.

In the summer of 1967 Lea had begun a second learning group, Hypnotherapy II, which was to follow patterns similar to those of her first. Work in the group was powerful, deep and safe. But with Lea's return from North Carolina in February 1968, an entirely different atmosphere, as one woman said, even "an entirely different person" took over the group. Lea asked people to speak of their feelings about her having been away. One woman felt a surge of rage toward Lea, occasioned by incidents of abandonment when a small child, but never emotionally experienced as an adult. Invited, she said what she was feeling though she was clearly terrified to do so. A few others brought forth similar feelings. As she would have done earlier, Lea made no attempt to place these feelings in a context for them. Rather she simply turned to the rest of the group asking, "Do you see what we're seeing here?" Frightened, others in the group turned on the speakers as pariah, accusing them of destructive intents. Lea didn't intervene or make any attempt to work with the material. Instead she ended the group session, leaving the speakers until the following week with the terrible burden of having been judged by Lea and the others as monsters. This woman recalled,

> "The sense that we were left with was that what we were feeling was dark, very dark, a hatred of the matrix (the mother). We were considered demonic. That week I was really scared, and I hoped that by the time we met again I wouldn't still have those feelings toward Lea. In the next group, she asked us how we were now feeling. I said that I did still have a bit of that feeling toward her. Actually, I had become quite self-destructive. I had turned against myself and was feeling physically ill. In the group people said all manner of things about me. Lea just sat there and said nothing. I don't know what the hell she was doing. There was no leadership. It was Kleiniann in a way." (A reference to theories that Melanie Klein elaborated after

an analysis of her own children). I guess she saw us as the children wanting to kill the mother."

The group stayed together until after Christmas but then it came apart. There was no longer the feeling that people had had in the earlier groups, of Lea coming in and rolling up her sleeves and getting down to work.

This woman had connected with powerful reactions to the death of her father when she was three, the subsequent troubles of her mother, and her mother's marriage less than a year later to a man who brought his own pastiche of problems into the young family. Lea herself had wounded places of this kind and after the Bigwin experience was much closer to them. However, she had no context wherein she was willing or able to surrender herself and to get help. As a result, there was a substantial change in her style of working. Earlier she would use an upsurge of early, primitive material in a client as a fulcrum to deeper resolution. Longings, terrible rages and terrors were all grist for the mill. Not only did she encourage clients to bring these feelings forward, but she would deftly work to reassure the individual that these were but the cries of a small child, not an indication of evil or of an unworkable pathology. But struggling to manage and subdue her own troubles, Lea retreated from this position. She could pick up and identify fear and rage in clients, but especially in groups she wasn't able to work with them as she had formerly. Her approach became more one of identifying this layer of material, labelling it, and distancing herself from it as from an infectious disease. It was at this period that she began to say that she could no longer work with people whom she classified as "paranoids."

Lea began to speak of paranoia at some length and about those who were paranoid, i.e., those who fomented internally with a desire to destroy the matrix, the mother, that is, Lea herself. The ironic piece here is that Lea had herself become "paranoid," i.e., frightened of the power of feelings that her work had stirred in others and in herself. The identified "paranoid" others became for her a present-day embodiment of the, until then successfully repressed, fears that she had held since a young child. A men's group begun earlier, was shut down. Men who had worked with her as clients, as learners, and as colleagues in the development of the farm became divided into two groups: those who were with her, that is, who didn't challenge her centrality, and, those who held opinions contrary to her own. Especially in the first decade of Therafields, it would be a misnomer to assert that there was an actual Group opposed to Lea. Rather there existed individuals who were unhappy with some of her pronouncements and decisions. They might or might not speak of these in the seminar. If they were to do so, Lea and her 'assistants' could challenge the individual in ways that rendered the challenge, as well as the challenger, impotent. The speaker would be found to be revealing problems he had with his father or his mother. (I designate 'he' advisedly, as it was mainly a few men from the former Catholic group who would reveal their displeasure.) There might be jokes or there might be unpleasant accusations made against the upstart. The rest would sit quietly, unwilling to join in the melee.

I don't wish to imply that after this period Lea was incapable of doing deeper work with clients. In smaller group settings or with individuals she continued to do so. But something powerfully significant had happened to cause her to back away from areas where before she had courageously gone. Meg, who was part of Lea's entourage for over a decade, spoke of the way that as Lea's health deteriorated in the late 1970s, she could not bear to be alone.

> "That was already happening in 1968 though it wasn't as obvious. That's why she had us with her. Sometimes late at night she would have someone massage her. It became obvious that she simply didn't want to be alone. She often slept with the light on."

From 1968 Lea rarely, if ever, took a group by herself. Invariably she would bring someone with her, sometimes several people, people specially chosen to "assist" her, people who would never contradict or take an opposite perspective from hers either in or out of the group. They would defend Lea and her positions in groups and in meetings.

In pointing to the Bigwin experience as central to the breakdown of Lea's defences, I also don't want to suggest that without Bigwin this would not have happened. I think that something of this nature was inevitable given the trajectory of Lea's situation and that of the existing community.

But still, Bigwin was a large, identifiable turning point. The break-down of her defences and the building of new ones with the resultant changes in Lea's relationships did not happen all at once. It was a process that was accelerated by Bigwin, coincident with her failing health, her need to take care of herself, and her desire for greater personal satisfaction. By the time Lea returned from North Carolina there were demonstrable changes. These cannot be attributed simply to the idea that Lea had made up her mind to take care of herself and to live differently. The changes went too deep for that conclusion. Many threads came together during this period: the loss of earlier physical and emotional defences and the rebuilding of others, her attraction to and involvement with Visvaldis, her guilt and worry about her children, and her desire to bring them into the communal fold to get help for them. These became central concerns for her that shaped much of her subsequent involvement with Therafields and with the directions that it took.

The Willow, Harry, and Visvaldis

In the summer of 1968 Visvaldis became a regular visitor at the farm. He wasn't engaged as were the rest of us in the on-going development and up-keep of the place, but his presence was felt, particularly in anything to do with construction. He designed and was a consultant on the building of a new vestibule entrance. In August, Lea and Harry purchased a farm down the road from Therafields. Lea engaged Visvaldis whose architectural work favoured a distinctly Frank Lloyd Wright element, to consult on the renovations that she wanted. That farm was called by her "The Willow" after a large willow tree in the yard. She and Harry moved from 59 Admiral Road to the Willow though Lea rented an apartment where she could stay in Toronto for her sessions and groups. This was the first occasion that she had a residence separate from her family and her clients/colleagues.

Harry had come from Yorkshire, sporting a common-man's accent different from Lea's more patrician lilt. Around the pre- and early Therafields community he was an anomalous being, a fellow at home with other working-class guys, enjoying a good laugh and a beer, but seemed an unusual consort to the head lady. Visvaldis was about 17 years Lea's junior but this did not seem to be an issue. Lea was more concerned about the impact an open separation from Harry and an alliance with Visvaldis would have on the community of people who looked to her as a teacher and guide. It was not spoken of openly except among those close to the couple and only gradually did it become common knowledge. As late as the summer of 1969 Lea and Visvaldis and a few others chose to stay at a motel when visiting Jim Healy's cottage in Connecticut because of the scandal it might cause to some of us who were also there if she and Visvaldis were seen to be cohabiting.

With the advent of Visvaldis another important element entered into the development of Therafields, though his influence on Lea was not immediately felt by those of us once removed from her closer circle. I became aware of his presence and his relationship to her only gradually, mainly seeing him at the farm and especially at the Willow. I remember my first introduction to him. Two of my housemates and I were camping at Wasaga Beach one weekend late in the summer of 1967. Visvaldis came up to our tent and spoke to Don whom he had met at the Prudhomme marathon earlier that spring. Don introduced us. I remember the assured manner with which Visvaldis appraised me and the smooth, jocular way in which he spoke. I could feel his charm, but I didn't particularly like him. He seemed to me somewhat dangerous, a con man. By the time I next saw him over a year later, Visvaldis and Lea had developed a relationship that remained central to both for the rest of their lives.

Lea and Visvaldis had clearly seen things in each other that they wanted and needed. Lea had married a man for whom responsibility was not a major suit. Harry was out of his depth in the things his wife was getting into. Visvaldis had perhaps a greater sense of responsibility but had a great deal of trouble following through and finishing things he started. He worried a lot about it, but he was a deeply conflicted man. A lot of how he spent his time shows how he was a kid trying to get away from being an adult. Still, as Meg K reflected, "Visvaldis was charismatic enough himself that the two of them could waltz off into a charismatic aura and manage for some time to keep enough of a semblance of reality that they didn't fall off the ledge."

There was never much common knowledge about Visvaldis, where he had come from (other than that he was Latvian), or what he had done prior to his coming to Therafields. In the years from 1967 until his death in 1983, I believe that his only architectural clients were Lea and Therafields. He encouraged Lea to view herself as a Grand Dame and to aspire to a patrician life that marriage to Harry had "denied" her. His counsel, opinions, and needs became a central facet of her life and her decisions. Visvaldis had expansive ideas about building for the new millennium, but when it came to men and women he was very patriarchal. Lea had been more advanced about the roles of women before he came along, but afterwards those ideas collapsed and disappeared. Snide comments would be made about people who didn't conform to gender roles. These would not be made by Lea herself, to my knowledge. In the main they came from Rob and Barrie.

Visvaldis designed renovations of the Willow that over the years transformed its original farmhouse into a Frank Lloyd Wright-inspired mansion. When it became clear that the work being done there was prohibitively expensive, an idea was sold to the working therapists that the house was being remodelled to be more than just Lea's home: it was to be a refuge for seminar members at the farm conducting marathons with their clients, and, a space to hold larger-scale marathons for the learning groups. This transformed concept allowed a financial sleight of hand whereby the costs of renovation and upkeep of the Willow shifted from Lea's personal responsibility to that of Therafields itself. With this rationale, the Willow was developed over several years at the financial expense of the working therapists and with their labour and that of their clients. As Rob, Barrie, and the Therafields' accountant Rik Day were responsible for buying and selling properties and establishing financial priorities, sweet deals like this were easy and essentially unknown to the community members, likely to most, if not all members of the seminar as well. Visvaldis received room and board at the Willow as well as a salary.

Beginning of construction at the Willow's

Digging out the basement

Mural in the basement by Jerome McNichol

The Willow as it grew

Visvaldis on site

Lea's Life and Roles Post-North Carolina

In his book *The Rise and Fall of Lea Hindley-Smith's Therafields Commune*, Grant Goodbrand makes a general statement about Lea's return from North Carolina. As she more openly showed her relationship with Visvaldis, it was made apparent to the men in Hypno I that

> "she had a consort and was very sexual. There was now an alpha male in their midst, a situation they had previously avoided. There was competitiveness, jealousy, hostility and criticism, as well as a desire to unseat and exclude Visvaldis, all of the typical power struggles, amounting to a classic Oedipal complex." (pg. 100)

However, a consort is not necessarily an alpha male. Visvaldis did not at any time have, or probably even want, the position of an alpha male in Therafields. The alpha male, for example in a wolf pack, is the one who grabs an up-start by the scruff of the neck and beats him into submission. There were never contests of this kind with Visvaldis. He did not take people on in an authoritative manner. He was simply Lea's partner. Some people liked him, and some didn't. Some enjoyed his capabilities and his personality but when others didn't like him, it had more to do with Visvaldis himself and ways that he behaved that were found offensive. He made some good contributions and had some good qualities. He could also be arrogant and sometimes was a predator of sexually vulnerable young women. Lea loved and protected Visvaldis. She gave him a forum in which to do some work. But by the same token she gave him an arena in which to act out his own fantasies. She wanted her partner to be happy. For that he needed work and he needed money. To get these things for him Lea had to subject aspects of the developing life of Therafields to those ends and to blind herself to the games that he was playing with some of its members.

In any wolf pack, there is not just an alpha male; there is a corresponding alpha female. She is the only one allowed to have pups. She will fight and discipline the others, subduing them into subservience and into the roles of caring for her and her pups. This was a space that Lea herself began to take up as the changes in herself and in Therafields unfolded in 1967-9. It was obvious to Lea that she could no longer continue in the role as head therapist. The numbers were too great, and the community had become too complex. She needed to carve out another space for herself, one that did not forego the centrality of her former position. When she came back to Toronto, Lea was no longer in a weakened state. She was stronger than she had been in years after a couple of months of R&R, good food, long walks and yoga, as well as considerable weight loss. She used that strength to assert herself. Lea gradually settled into the role of Teacher, a role that over time was delineated as both unique and unassailable. During the next several years she would reflect upon and speak of issues of concern to herself and push for them to be "worked with" communally through the learning groups and the seminar. The following is an example of the ways that Lea transformed herself from therapist to Teacher and Leader during that first year back from North Carolina.

Grant writes of the series of meetings that Lea had shortly after her return with a men's group that she had formed from the Hypnotherapy group. It was disbanded after these meetings Lea then spoke openly in different settings about the group saying that it had been unworkable due to its core of destructive, woman-hating material. In the meetings, Grant reports that Lea demanded that the men

> "speak honestly about their resistance to the changes in her and their feelings about Visvaldis. She also pressed them about their feelings about women having control over their own bodies and sexuality and independence in their personal values and choices." (pg. 101)

Aware that there was discomfort among the members of the seminar about her relationship, Lea went aggressively on the offensive. Each of the issues that she flagged for discussion was related to her own situation and struggle. Would she be allowed to control her own body, sexuality, and independence of values and choices? This wasn't just about "women" in general, this was very much about herself. Having discussions of this nature would have been excruciatingly difficult for that group of men as so much could not be spoken of honestly. Most had had awareness over the preceding year not only of her relationship with Visvaldis, but also of the way that it had come about. They knew that Visvaldis had been, and perhaps still was in some manner, Lea's client. They also knew that Visvaldis' wife, a member of Lea's group, and Harry, Lea's husband whom most knew quite well, had been put aside. These men owed much to Lea and in the main wanted very much to support her. But in this instance, being loyal to her and true to their own values were in conflict.

As the meetings continued Lea confronted the men about their hatred of women, a theme to which she was to return often. Viewing the movie Zorba the Greek had crystallized for her a belief that the sources of discomfort she discerned in the seminar were similar to those that had driven the men of a village to hound and murder a beautiful young widow for the crime of freely-enjoyed sexuality. These sources Grant cites as: "male entitlement to control women, the hatred of a woman's freedom, the envy of her creative gifts, and primitive violence." (pg. 101)

It is true that these elements have existed in all cultures for millennia. We all have grown up in a patriarchal society, absorbing the language and attitudes of its culture. But there are widely different ways that these are displayed and acted out from one society to another. Certainly, this group of men had within themselves, to varying degrees, attitudes detrimental to women. Lea was touching on real elements of the patriarchy. But she was not going there primarily to promote an understanding of these issues. Rather it was done as a method of control. It was a finger pointed at the men. Lea herself, like all of us, had absorbed many of the same views and attitudes though she enacted them in different ways. In the meetings, she challenged the men aggressively and individually about their feelings, especially as they related to Visvaldis and herself. She singled out each and "worked with" him searching for the way that his negative feelings manifested themselves. While this happened, the others would be silent. She was their teacher and their therapist, the woman with whom they still had strong transferences. They were not about to collectively or individually stand up to her and say, "What the hell are you doing?" They had to listen and to acknowledge that there was some truth in what she said. But she humiliated them; she reduced them.

This is how the alpha figure will operate. I will show my power over you and you will be careful after that. The conversation might have been about the patriarchal discourse but that was only the content. The inherent message was, "I have the power to interpret events and feelings; I am the one who will tell you how things really are." This approach cannot be called therapeutic. No wonder the group was unworkable. As Grant recalls, it was a traumatic experience for some of the men. It stirred terrible feelings for these guys, very confusing feelings. They had respected her, in many cases loved her, and had worked hard for her while she was away. Now she was asserting power over them while discussing her new relationship in a manner not forthcoming or honest. Given their histories with Lea it was difficult for any to protest or to take a consistent stand against her. It wasn't in their natures or hearts to band together a counter group against the directions that she was taking.

I question Grant's assertion that after these meetings the men of the Hypnotherapy group changed their attitudes and ways of dealing with women. In my experience, most were decent in their friendships with women colleagues and their relations with women clients. They were not exactly a bunch of red-necks and they certainly weren't Greek villagers. The real outcome of the meetings was a marking of Lea's position and a growing estrangement between her and some of the men who had formerly been among her greatest supporters. Men singled out and gone after in this manner would experience it as a profound betrayal. But I don't believe Grant's conclusion that the essence of the estrangement derived from an Oedipal struggle. These men were not collectively four-year old to the adult parents, Lea and Visvaldis. In relation to Lea they were, if anything, more like adolescents who had enjoyed close relations with an encouraging mother. They were growing into some confidence as therapists. While she was away they had had to shoulder much and were ready to continue doing so. After years with, for all intents and purposes, a "single" mom, she had taken a boyfriend under circumstances that they didn't entirely understand and weren't comfortable with. And they weren't exactly crazy about him or about the ways she was bringing him into everything. None of their responses would be surprising. Because of her own insecurity, Lea couldn't simply allow things to be as there were, to just let Visvaldis and the others gradually regularize their relationships. The meetings were comparable on a broader scale to a mother accusing her teenage boy of harbouring murderous feelings towards her and her new beau because the boy wasn't happy with the changes in the household. Confused? Distraught? Estranged? Definitely. All the above.

Lea was no freer than the men whom she confronted from the attitudes and actions of patriarchy. Her own ways of dealing with women in fact fit well within the patriarchal schemata. I don't think that she was at ease being on equal terms with other women. She had no actual women friends. Those with whom she surrounded herself after her return from North Carolina tended to have histories of caring for adults from their early years and these proclivities were exploited as they came into Lea's sphere. They became her caretakers. They looked after her: cooking, cleaning, caring for her clothes and hair, giving her massages, in the mid-1970s assisting with her writing, and in the late 1970s, early 1980s, providing nursing and custodial care. These women were not colleagues, friends or equals and they were no longer clients. They had been co-opted into traditional patriarchal roles of handmaidens to the leader.

Other women who did not enter into caretaking roles with her were kept in line by other means. The Tuesday-Friday group had been taken in Lea's absence by Janet G. Janet worked differently than Lea. The pace was not the same, but the work was good. In the late spring or early summer of 1968, the group had a weekend marathon at the farm. Lea did what became a feature of her "supervision" of her former groups: she dropped in from time to time. On the first instance that Lea came to the group with Janet, she sat quietly allowing Janet to proceed. After a while, she interrupted saying, "Wait. This is very superficial. This isn't getting down to things." She proceeded to take over the session, in the process humiliating Janet publicly, shocking and confusing the rest of us. She made it clear to Janet and to us that she was the only one who could be relied upon to know what were appropriate therapeutic directions. I experienced in that setting the kind of estrangement from Lea that Grant identified in the men of the Hypnotherapy group. I had had a great deal of respect and admiration for her. I had not by any means always found her gentle, but she had been very tuned in and a deep worker. From around that time in 1968, I began to feel that there was someone else present, someone confusing and unpredictable.

'Threshold Therapy'

I remember that year of 1968 being one of great instability. With Lea unwell and away, there was a sense of insecurity within the community as a whole. Would she survive her illness? What would happen to the community if she did not? These ideas were never spoken of in the context that I was a part of, but they were felt nonetheless. The inner group of more mature people, with whom I had lived for my first year and a half at 32 Admiral Road, had moved early that year over to 55 and 59 Admiral, forming part of the new Hypnotherapy group. In their places had come neophytes, people working with newer therapists, with no experience or connection with Lea nor of Lea with them. I was sharing a room in the basement with another new member but was still affiliated with the third floor. I was now considered one of the 'elders,' someone who could be helpful in this new dispensation. We no longer had regular house groups. If we had, they were taken by different people from the seminar who didn't have the histories and connections with us that Lea had had. I have clear memories of the quality of the house groups we had with Lea each Sunday morning, but none of the groups held once the new people arrived. It was a time of chaos. Things were happening on the third floor that would never have been tolerated when Lea was our therapist and people like Tom, Don, and Bernice lived with us. One or two people regularly got drunk and acted in ways that were frightening to others. A few people had tantrums, throwing things about, breaking dishes. Things were out of control and there was no one solid to turn to.

When Lea had returned from North Carolina, there was, of course, a general sense of relief that she was well, in fact much healthier than before, but nothing went back to the way it had been. Lea no longer regularly took her standard groups. At some point that year she decided to move

63

people who had been in her standard groups but who were now in house groups, out of the former, situating the main focus of their therapies within the house groups. She based this decision on ideas that she was working with at the time. These ideas were not necessarily grounded in the reality of their effects. By this period, Lea was simply too removed from the day-to-day experience of house group living in the extended Therafields milieu to realize the actual impact of the changes. She was talking in different contexts at that time about the work done in house groups as being 'threshold therapy,' and what she called Theradrama, as her unique contribution to the evolution of psychotherapy. She wanted henceforth to underscore this 'breakthrough,' by having the therapists call themselves 'theradramists,' and their clients, 'dramists.'

By 'Theradrama' Lea meant the way in which people emotionally reconstitute their families of origin within a group context, seeking to replay their early conflicts or longings. Therapy conducted in that setting and with that understanding can enable a person to recognize and resolve patterns. Out of her talks an edict came forth changing the nature of house group life as Lea had originally viewed it. This shift laid pressures on the house group context that in many cases it could not bear. Earlier a distinction had been made between standard groups and house groups. It was said that the deeper therapy took place in the standard groups, whereas house groups were helpful for learning patterns that one should take to their therapist and their group. It wasn't seen as deeper therapy when people got together as a house group. It was to be a space to deal with practical matters and with issues about getting along with others. That changed when Lea decided that house groups were the places that the deeper therapy should be taking place. People left their standard groups, but many of the house groups didn't become more stable or safe. Interviews that I had with people who became part of the community after 1968 revealed to me some of the variations of experiences that were had once house groups were considered not simply a healthy living experiment, but a central component of therapeutic activity.

June K (a pseudonym) who had come to Toronto at the behest of her brother, told me of living in an Admiral Road house around 1970. Houses were by then being clumped together into 'milieus,' groupings of three-to-five houses in which people in a common learning group, for example, would be interactive. Milieu group meetings were thus large and unwieldy. Pressures might be released but the process could not be considered therapeutic. Though she found her experience interesting and even exciting, it seemed to her that she had lived during that period in a circus atmosphere, always with a certain feeling of dread.

Living at 123-5 Walmer Road in the early 1970s was, for Rob P, a confusing and overwhelming experience. There seemed to have been an implied expectation for the 25 house members to eat their suppers together in the basement common room. In such a relatively small space, tensions could easily give rise to upset, even to screaming and violence. Therapists for the house groups rotated, so there was little consistency or security. As he recalled, "People would go wild and were encouraged to go wild. Dinner would stop and there would be a big group with someone pounding pillows in the living room."

With the focus on house groups as primary sites for therapy, a more contained context of a single house group of 12-15 people was workable for some, though the outcomes depended greatly on the readiness of each member to work emotionally there, as well as the skill and personal quality of the therapist. David B moved into a smaller house group on Walmer Road around 1973. Those living there were quite similar in age and maturity. Most had their feet on the ground and had jobs. He found that the therapy work done was quite raw.

> "Jim Healy was the therapist. and he was excellent. He was
> dedicated and thorough. He had to open himself to be
> able to work so deeply with people. I felt very safe in that
> house group no matter what went on, mainly because of
> him and because of two of the other members with whom
> I had become close."

David believed that difficulties in the house group arose from people who were not willing to participate on an emotional level. They might want to control or avoid the group dynamic, but they were not going to participate. David was puzzled that therapists put people like that into house groups.

In David's next group house experience at 123-5 Walmer, the larger venue was taken by a pair of therapists. There he believes that he grew more by becoming aware of the overall subtext of the house dynamics than by any direct therapeutic interventions. He saw that a hierarchical atmosphere that had become more a feature of life throughout Therafields by the early 1970s, was affecting the atmosphere of the house group. Though he recognized the brilliance of the female therapist and the energy and dedication of the male therapist, he 'couldn't buy the routine.' It was very strict – "my way or the highway." David found that, unlike in his earlier group with Jim, the house group meetings were not the place to speak of contrary opinions. In his view, the dynamic was basically centred on the therapists. However, he believes that this experience helped him to understand the politics of how things worked within the community.

> "If you saw something going on and spoke of it, something that might run counter to the accepted ideas about Lea, the therapists, or Therafields, for example, you could be told that it was your own paranoia. Then you would walk around feeling crazy."

My brother, Craig, had come into therapy a year or so after me. He worked with Ken P for a time and was in the group that Ken co-facilitated with his then wife, Marion. When Craig moved to St Catharines to get his BA degree from Brock University, he left therapy though continued a few years later, working for years with Peter D. When we spoke later of his experiences, Craig stressed the emphasis placed on confrontation in groups in the early 1970s. The nature of this approach pushed many people into their defences or helped them to build new ones: "how to talk the talk." In the mid-1960s Lea had made a great issue about the dangers, evils even, of conformity, but whole new layers and forms of conformity were just a few years later taking hold. Craig recalled:

> "What crept in was a certain sense that there was a way to be in the world and if you weren't that way there was something wrong with you and you'd better get your shit

together fast. People would go after one another in the groups. There was a high predominance of the super-ego."

In his first house group on Walmer Road there were what he called 'real flag-wavers' who took over the group, using guilt and shaming as methods of control. There was pressure to work at the farm or on other current projects, to be and to eat in a certain way. Eat this and wash it in this way. It seemed to him that everyone was terrified but was trying to look like they were alright. He listened to all the stuff about food, for example, and thought, "I'm going to starve here. It was all so precious and contrived." The focus on food and its preparation stemmed directly from various fads with which Lea herself was experimenting during this period. Macrobiotics was a big draw for awhile, as was fasting for short or longer periods, and digestive problems with eating starch and protein in the same meal were highlighted.

In his next house group, Craig found people more able to "drop the mask of being 'OK' and just be human with one another." His third experience, however, was in a larger setting. There he found more extreme examples of manipulation by guilt and shame, and of conformity to idealized notions of how one ought to be. He did not feel free to express his thoughts and feelings. "There were about 40 people there and no real therapy ever seemed to happen. I thought that it was my problem because I just couldn't get it." Many of the women living there appeared to him quite troubled, though none of their issues seemed to be addressed in the groups. He didn't feel secure enough to deal directly with what he felt while there. The size of the group and the sense of himself as an outsider kept him from talking about his own issues. He was afraid of the male therapist and didn't trust the woman. To Craig she appeared too concerned about herself as a guru. She was flippant in the groups; she didn't seem to take things seriously. Craig didn't think that the work in the groups was good. It always looked like something was happening but none of it sat right with him. After a year or so of frustration in this setting, he left despite a strong effort of others to get him to stay. He never regretted having left though he found the process of doing so difficult and painful.

The experiences of these people show some of the elements of the Therafields milieu between about 1968-75. The initial fragmentation of house group responsibility from Lea to a host of others left many groups in a state of confusion and even outright chaos. The size of the groups often militated against the necessary sense of contained safety needed for good therapy to occur, especially in situations wherein several households were combined to form a 'milieu.' Groups then could contain up to 40 or 50 people. Also, Lea's thrust toward confrontation in groups after 1968, which eventually extended down into the standard groups and house groups, often led to a stifling dose of the super-ego and new forms of conformity. The decision in 1968 to move the main focus of deeper therapy from standard to house groups in many instances merely increased pressures experienced by people already overwhelmed by the intensity of their house group experiences. On the other hand, by 1975 some of the therapists who had begun working with clients between 1966 and 1970 had developed considerable experience with both groups and individuals and were able to do good work independently.

In her earlier practice, Lea had not espoused a communal philosophy. She made clear to her clients that the goal was for them to do their therapy work and then to get on with their lives. This approach changed as Lea became more involved and invested (as did we right along with her) in the proliferation of house groups and learning groups. Drawing back from the nitty-gritty of daily slog in the therapeutic trenches, Lea developed terminology and concepts to frame her view of what she and Therafields were then about. But theory is a double-edged sword. You find a box and then try to squeeze everything into it. Some things simply won't fit; so like the heels and toes of Cinderella's less charming step-sisters, they are squeezed, distorted, or simply lopped off. The house group idea was indeed a special innovation of Lea's own. It gave a grounded environment for many who had been living relatively impoverished lives isolated in a large city. I, like many of my contemporaries, found the house group milieu lived as Lea originally set it up, safe and nourishing. But living that way provided the seed of the ultimate extension of therapy into a way of life rather than simply a passage into a fuller life of one's own. Most of us found ourselves for the first time living closely with other people with whom we could share deeply not just our troubles but also our interests and joys. Possibilities abounded for lasting friendships and for mating. How was one to leave such a life behind? We stayed on, moving with the stream of events as they unfolded over the years, not fully understanding, any more than Lea herself understood fully, the multiplicity of desires and needs that both kept us there and that propelled us along the paths that Therafields eventually took.

We gained in diverse ways from being there, but also remained in a kind of time warp, staying adolescent, children to Lea's "Momma." Lea gained many things as well, but some of these were not good for her. The position that she carved out for herself gave her power that was ultimately destructive to the very principles that she had prided herself on in her early years as a therapist. The blurring of boundaries led easily to the reaping of "secondary gains," no longer so much a danger to be avoided, but a way of life not only for herself but for those closest to her, the "family" whom she so wanted to redeem.

Writing about Lea and Therafields is like trying to encompass every dimension of a hologram at the same moment. There were simply so many variables, so many contradictory but nonetheless true things happening all at once. One might say, "This was going on," but almost immediately would have to qualify that statement with another: "AND, this was happening as well." This is how it was in Therafields from its beginning.

The Character Analysis Group (CAG)

In the fall of 1968 Lea founded a third learning group, taking its name from the title of Wilhelm Reich's major opus, Character Analysis. Most of those joining this new group were, like me, people who had come into therapy around 1966, and who had been seeing the new therapists from Lea's Hypnotherapy Group. When Tom, at that point my therapist, asked me if I was interested in being a part of CAG, I was eager to join. I was more and more interested in learning to be a psychotherapist. Besides, I didn't like the idea of being left behind. In October 1968, the proposed members met for an initial marathon weekend at the farm. There were over 80 of us. I found the experience overwhelming but had no intention of not continuing.

Lea had become interested in Reich's work through Alexander Lowen's book on bioenergetics, *The Betrayal of the Body*. But physical work was only one part of the orientation that she wished to take with this and subsequent learning groups. "The way that we worked in the Hypnotherapy group is too slow," she said. "I want you people to go more directly after defences, to learn how to confront these by doing it here in the group." Reich's approach was not the verbal confrontation Lea was espousing, however. His work was looking at bodily defences, identifying and making his patients aware of muscular blocks, places of tension, and shallow breathing. He saw that from an early age a person could develop specific tensions to prevent him or herself from feeling painful or frightening emotions. These tensions became chronic adaptations. He found that putting tight muscles under stress and opening-up a person's breathing could release tension and liberate the emotional substrata. Reich would have a patient breathe more deeply, allowing a greater flow of energy throughout the body. Sometimes this work would lead to spontaneous crying or rage. Memories might surface that would make clearer the sources of the tensions.

Reich grew up on his father's extensive farm estate in Galicia where as a child he raised and studied animals. He served in the Austro-Hungarian army during WWI in Italy, later attending medical school and becoming a neuro-psychiatrist. Reich met Freud in Vienna while still a medical student. He quickly became a part of Freud's group of colleagues, beginning work in Freud's "ambulatory" clinic and becoming an important member of the psychoanalytic community. His approach went to the heart of Freud's early contention that neuroses were caused by sexual disturbances. Reich became convinced that the frustration of energy in the human body, held in by muscular armouring, was the prime source of physical and mental illness. Releasing energy through massage and specific exercises could allow a patient fuller experience of sexual orgasm, to Reich, the sine qua non of health. Working and teaching within the sexually repressive society of the early 20th century, Reich turned his attention to social questions, advocating birth control, abortion, divorce, and adolescent sexuality. It was he who coined the phrase, "the sexual revolution," an eventual societal development aided by his many publications and by the spread of his techniques for freeing energy.

Reich was a fiery, passionate believer in his approach. He experimented with methods of measuring energy fields in the human body, as well as ways to draw and accumulate energy from the earth's atmosphere. This "orgone" energy, as he called it, was used to augment a patient's lower levels of energy by placing him or her in a box in which orgone had been "gathered." His views, radical for the era, and his unusual methodology alienated many from his work. Ultimately, he was disbarred from the Vienna Psychoanalytic Society. Reich moved to Norway, then to the United States, just before the outbreak of World War II. There he taught at the New University of New York, continued to publish theories that related all forms of illness to the repression of sexual energies, and developed more elaborate orgone receptors for the treatment of his patients.

A magazine article critical of his methods alerted the US Food and Drug Administration to his work. Suspecting him of being a charlatan, the Administration imposed restrictions on the transportation of his "boxes" and his books across state lines. The energy accumulation process occurred in Maine, an area that Reich had found ideal for the work. Boxes were then taken to New York for use. One of his co-workers took boxes and books despite the order. He and Reich were accused and convicted of contempt of court, and Reich was sentenced to two years in prison. His orgone boxes were impounded and destroyed and about six tons of his books were burned by order of the court. After his appeals were exhausted, Reich entered prison in 1957, dying that fall of heart failure.

Reich undoubtedly pioneered important theories about the functioning of the human body, as well as methods of releasing energy holding back physical and mental health. How he has been seen historically is dependent upon the perspective of the viewer and the segment of Reich's work that is under review. His later work, especially experimenting with energy collectors, did not survive his death in any significant manner. However, his techniques of working directly with the body of a patient spawned myriad ways of connecting with deeper strata of repressed emotional material, especially if used in conjunction with the earlier "talk therapy" of Freud.

It was very interesting work, an important innovation. Lea incorporated this aspect of Reich's work by having John N. begin bioenergetic groups in the summer of 1969 with the men and the women of both the seminar and of CAG. In these groups, we followed exercises that Dr. John Pierrakos and Alexander Lowen had learned from Reich. John's groups were held at first in his room at 70 Walmer Road, later in a small bio-energetic room built in the basement of 310 Dupont Avenue in Toronto's Annex area, and still later in the larger bio-rooms constructed when 316 Dupont was purchased. John had four groups: two for the men of the seminar and of CAG, the other two for the women.

I was eager, if nervous, beginning this quite raw work. I had recognized clearly the year before when reading Lowen's book that I would benefit from his techniques. There were about 10 women from CAG who met with John at 70 Walmer. We would begin with a series of exercises that would stretch different sets of muscles to the point that they would vibrate, and our bodies would shake. It was rather comical to see but was an important part of Reich's approach – putting muscles under stress, forcing them to release held-in feelings. John had "Lowen stools" constructed for our use. Bending backward over one of these at the shoulder blade level and with arms extended backward over one's head, would deepen our often-shallow breathing. During this and other exercises like hitting a mat with a tennis racket, punching an upright mat, or stomping about the room shouting, "NO" or "YES," would often lead to spontaneous crying or angry outbursts by one or another member. When this happened, all of us would focus on her, sometimes acting out a drama that was touched on from her earlier life. It was very powerful work and shook many of us deeply. It also brought us closer together and forged deeper bonds of trust and friendship. Some stayed with this work and grew with it. Some found it too intense or scary for themselves at the time.

In the meantime, Meg K. had become a registered masseuse, using that modality as a further complement to expressive therapy, and others from CAG, including me, followed her to the massage college. About ten people engaged in physical work, developing it as a central focus in their practices. For the other 70 or so group members, CAG was simply another learning group with a focus on confrontation. Of the people whom I interviewed from that group, only one man said that he had liked and learned from the Character Analysis Group. Many of us gained greatly from it in the sense that over the years we developed quite deep connections with one another and participated in work, play, and friendships together at the farm and in the city, that were in the broad sense therapeutic and wholesome.

But the groups themselves were often agonizing. Up to 80 people would sit on the floor in a room with the expectation that someone would confront and someone else would be confronted. One never knew when a group member might bring up a personal discontent directed at oneself. Lea preached from time to time that confrontation should not be done out of personal spite. One ought to do it only out of love, she would say, because you care about a person and want to help him or her. Good in theory, but in the real world more often it was those less in touch with their own vulnerabilities and those who enjoyed hearing themselves (or having Lea hear them) who would do the confronting. Unquestionably, personal irritations and enmities were sometimes at work. Those not on the "hot seat" would hide, hoping to be overlooked. One member spoke to me of the way that she lived in fear and trembling of those groups. "I remember feeling that you could do something completely innocently and then get lambasted for it."

Lea's presumption then was that those of us in the learning groups had pretty much completed our own therapy work and were now ready for a crisper give and take. This was far from the truth. For me, being there felt too much like "family meetings" where as a kid, I could suddenly be scolded and humiliated in front of the others. I spent a lot of the time in CAG groups keeping a low profile, sitting in places where I would not be especially visible.

After 1968, Lea encouraged the reading of several of Reich's books, taking whole-cloth swaths of his preaching for her own. From Reich, she adopted the powerful notion of "the emotional plague," a concept central to the elaborations of theories that characterized her "teachings" in the 1970s. Therapy became less about "opening people up to their glorious selves" – Lea's earlier Rousseau-like spin on the essential goodness of people – and became more a search for the hidden depths of darkness that lurked within. Lea was closing in some essential manner. Her own unresolved fears, certainly by the mid-1970s, led her to dwell upon those who might destroy her or her creation, "Therafields."

As in the springtime 1968 Tuesday-Friday marathon at the farm where Lea had put Janet in her place, I observed her aggressively asserting her position in a late winter or early spring marathon in 1969 for the CAG learning group. During the 1968 Christmas break, Lea had convened a 'project,' a special small group to do therapy for up to several days focused on one person. This project was for Visvaldis. She asked Mike Quealey to be one of the workers. As the project progressed it became clear that there were difficulties in the relationship between Lea and Visvaldis and Mike addressed these. At a seminar meeting a week or so later, Lea furiously confronted Mike, calling him a saboteur. Visvaldis' problems had been fair territory but anything that implicated her as a problem was not. At CAG's subsequent marathon Lea missed a morning group and Mike took the chair. "Work" was done with a couple in the group who had been together for a year or so but who were having troubles. After a bit of talk Mike suggested that they might take a "moratorium," on their relationship -- i.e., step back a bit from the relationship and try to get clarity on what was happening. This suggestion was quite consistent with directions Lea

74

was taking at the time. She would decide that a relationship was not particularly healthy and would encourage that, usually the man, separate from his partner. The group ended, and we took a break.

After the break, Lea came back with Mike. She had had a report on the session and she was in a fury. She collectively grabbed not just Mike, but the entire group by the ears, giving all a good drubbing. How could Mike suggest such a destructive plan? Didn't he know that the woman in question had health issues and that she would DIE if her partner was taken from her? If we had agreed with Mike, how could we be so lacking in insight and compassion? If we had disagreed, why had we not challenged him? For the remainder of the session no further work was done with the couple, no insights or help were offered. Instead Lea spent the next hour and a half going around the circle of more than 80 people, forcing each to confess that he or she was either as deluded as Mike or else was too cowardly to confront him. Her energy and indignation were powerful. Mike sat quietly beside her during this process, head bowed, completely humiliated. In retrospect, I believe that Lea identified with the woman addressed by Mike, and that her fury came from what she considered his destructive intervention between Visvaldis and herself. Nonetheless it was a devastating occasion for one and all. Collectively we left that meeting with our tails tucked firmly between our legs. It was hideous but effective. Lea was clearly in charge.

Not long after CAG began, Lea invited some members, as she had done with the Hypnotherapy people in 1966, to try their hand at working with the constant overflow of new clients seeking therapists. Thereafter, the group gradually became a second seminar, joining the original seminar a couple of years later. In the seminar format the groups were not as threatening, though they could be boring. Sitting on the floor for an hour and a half hearing details of a problem client wasn't necessarily stimulating, especially in a room charged with unexpressed feelings and confusions. The amazing thing is that we stuck around. But we had committed so much by that time. Those of us who aspired to be therapists wanted to continue with the body work that we were learning. Also, many of us had histories with Lea in which good things had happened. We had to accommodate ourselves somehow. It became a relief when Lea wasn't at the group and increasingly, she was away. Many of us just learned to stay quiet and to get on with our lives in the diverse ways that we were developing. Some people did leave the group and eventually the community itself.

By May 1969 CAG had formed an identifiable group presence. Since the October marathon we had had meetings weekly in the basement of 59 Admiral, but the space was far too small to hold our numbers. In the winter a proposal had been advanced that we should purchase 310 Dupont St and convert it into group rooms and offices. CAG was to take the lead in raising money for this project as the Hypnotherapy Group had done for the farm. Like many of my fellow group members, I raised $500 by taking out a bank loan. The money was now considered to be shares in the general Therafields holdings. In May, Lea and her associates, very likely in the seminar, decided on another rearrangement of the house groups. CAG members who lived in various houses across the community would move in together at 55 and 59 Admiral. The following March we all moved again, over to Walmer Rd, an arrangement that lasted a brief six months before a move back to three houses on 'upper' Admiral Rd.

310 Dupont purchased by CAG on the right

At the Farm: 1970-73

In the years between 1970 and 1973 that the CAG milieu was on Admiral Road, a great deal was happening at the farm. The massive building projects to which I alluded earlier were underway. Lea and Harry's farm, the Willow, was entirely transformed. Lea had an apartment on the second floor and there were rooms there for Harry, Josie, and Jack King, who had been asked to be a companion to Harry. On the ground floor were rooms for Rob and for Barrie as well as a large entrance hall, a dining room, a good-sized kitchen and breakfast area. Off to one side of the kitchen and down a level was the spacious group room. In a basement wing were a room for Visvaldis and two rooms used for other guests. The interior and exterior of the house resembled in great detail homes developed and lived in by Frank Lloyd Wright, a connection I was astonished to see some years later when visiting his former home in Arizona. Stone and wood detailed the exterior and within, solid terra cotta, blue, and red colours of southwestern decor were everywhere.

At Therafields farm these influences could also be seen, as it took on new forms, becoming more functional and beautiful. All of us were involved quite heavily in these projects. An organic garden had been started at the farm after a couple of years of a regular kitchen garden. It was labour-intensive. Every weekend crowds came up from the city for group marathons, or to be involved in building, gardening, cooking, or in the care and up-keep of the properties. Early on, I was involved in every aspect of the work though gradually a group of us in CAG was charged with organizing the cooking each weekend. Stella, who had been working as Lea's right-hand woman for some years, had over-all responsibility for the Willow and the farm. Two women who lived at the farm, cared for its day-to-day needs, the week-day cleaning, ordering of food, and cooking for the farm group. There were other staff at the Willow for its maintenance. When Lea was in residence, its numbers were swollen by those who travelled with her – a number that began to grow as the years passed.

Some of the farm staff came from people who had been part of a months-long Willow project group that had begun in October 1971. Some of the group members stayed on after the project wound down and that phase of the Willow renovation and construction was concluded. Most had given up their city jobs to remain at the Willow and now wished to continue their close involvement with the farm and the Willow. Remuneration for these positions was modest: room and board as well as a small monthly stipend. Those who stayed on had their own reasons for doing so – a love of the country, a sense of safety in what had become their home, a commitment to Lea and/or the community as a whole, and possibly, an unclear idea of where life might take them if they were to pull away from the closeted life they had been living and move back to the life of regular jobs and house groups.

For most of us, involvement at the farm was a regular but partial activity. We had jobs that required our attention during the week. Also, those of us in the early learning groups had taken on clients whom we saw for sessions weekly or twice a week. Our involvements at the farm consisted of coming there for our own groups and of volunteering in the garden, on construction sites, or in the kitchen. A custom was established that members of a therapy marathon one weekend would help to provide staff for cooking and cleaning the following weekend. The organizers from CAG came regularly to the farm on Friday nights, staying until Sunday afternoon, to work with and direct the other volunteers. We became accustomed to the routine of caring for up to 200 people per weekend. It was steady work but often fun and satisfying. We got to meet and spend time with lots of interesting people. On Saturday evenings we would dance to music in the dining room or go out together to the local pub for drinks and music. The farm felt like it was ours because we spent so much time there and contributed such a lot to its functioning.

In the kitchen: the author, Mag, and Judy

A group at the farm for a marathon, out for a stroll during a break

Preparing the fields for sowing

Sorting vegetables

Forming a pond for swimming

Developing the upper loft of the barn for entertainments and meetings

In the organic garden

Music at the fire pit

A fair in the 1977, open to the public

The fair

At the Willow

It was never the same at the Willow. From the fall of 1967, we had done a lot of work fixing up the barn and the farm house for group use. After the Willow was purchased, it became another important work site as it went through various expansions and renovations. In the early 1970s, from time to time a call would come down to the city on a week-day afternoon, asking for workers for the job site or for a team of women to come up to the Willow to clean. Despite just being home from work a bunch of us would rally, grab a bite to eat, drive up to the Willow, and help where needed. There was a sense of obligation to help, especially when Lea called, as well as a feeling of being close to the "inner sanctum," --- allowed to clean up Lea's own area. However, there was never real comfort being there.

Learning group meetings took place at the Willow. We would have breaks between sessions there but spent the nights and took most of our meals at the farm. From time to time, Lea would cook a meal of fish and chips together with her helpers and we would eat outside on the Willow patio.

After my daughter, Elizabeth was born in October 1976, she and I would be given one of the rooms in the lower level of the Willow, when we came up for a marathon. I was never at ease staying there. There was an aura of unreality and tension that I could never quite identify but which I attributed to my own problems. Since, I have spoken with many others who had groups there or who worked or stayed there. My own discomfort was reflected in those of many with whom I conversed. Central to the tenor of life there was the state of the relationship between Lea and Visvaldis. Barrie's girl-friend and later wife, spent most weekends with him at the Willow for years. It was clear to her that everything that happened there rose and fell on Visvaldis' mood and needs. Sometimes he was very depressed and wouldn't come out of his room. Everyone would cluster around him. On Saturday nights there was the big dinner, the one-conversation dinner. That meant that the only two people who would talk would be Rob and Barry. They would chat and make jokes and try to keep something going.

At the farm the regular weekend menus were simple, even Spartan. Usually lunch consisted of a hearty soup and the famous "Lisa bread," a dense multi-grain bread made by a local woman. Supper might be baked potatoes, a salad, and perhaps a dessert. As Lea went through various dietary fads, these would be reflected in the menu. However, those of us working in the farm kitchen were aware that the foods requested and taken down the road to the Willow tended to be more select and varied. Foods consumed at the Willow were paid for out of the same financial pot as those at the farm, but there was a definite distinction about who got what.

During those years, we continued to meet often at the farm for marathon groups, especially for the week-long summer marathons. By 1973 the Hypno I seminar and CAG had marathons together as most of us by then were at least part-time working therapists. We would usually meet in the mornings, have a break in the afternoons for swimming at the ponds at the farm or at the Phoenix farm, and then meet again in the late afternoon and after supper. These meetings took place at the Willow in the large group room. Lea would sit at the bottom of one set of stairs on a chair. A few of her inner circle would sit in chairs with her – often Rob and Barrie, sometimes Josie or Adam. The rest of us would arrange ourselves on cushions about the room: some in the deep area by the stone fireplace, some around the periphery, and others on the second set of stairs or on the landing at the top. Lea would often introduce some issues that were of interest to her and try to provoke discussion related to these ideas or themes. Periodically some dynamic work would take place with an individual, but usually it was just talk.

The themes that interested Lea at the time varied considerably. For example, since her return from South Carolina in 1968 she had focused a great deal on issues of health. This led her in many directions, not all of them sound. At the clinic Lea had been put on a regimen of diet and exercise, the usual treatment for her condition, and it was successful. She lost weight and got her blood sugar levels under control. What made her situation difficult though, was not simply this illness. Over time its control was stymied by problems that Lea already had relating more to her psychological and mental health. Lea's father had been hospitalized for years before his death after "descending into madness."

When a young woman, Lea feared that a similar fate could await her. She had asked Mike, her therapist in England, if she could have inherited some aspect of her father's disturbance. He assured her that such ideas were just old wives' tales. In truth, the greater the degree of consanguinity with a person with a mental health condition, the greater is the possibility of developing it. In that era, psychoanalysts were attempting to understand all forms of mental or psychological disorders as stemming from one's family history, from the "nurture" side of the nature/nurture dyad. Little was known at the time about the interactions of one's genetic inheritance and one's psychological history.

Lea sometimes spoke about periods of profound depression that she had suffered as a child and as a young woman. Again, this condition was not understood as a complex syndrome involving cognitive, physiological, and mood disorder symptoms. Depression of this nature can be triggered by a genetic predisposition as well as by damage done to brain functioning by extreme stress in early childhood.

When others spoke in groups of depression, she would tell stories of her own experiences. She was so paralyzed in one episode, she said, she had been barely able to rouse herself from her bed to care for her distraught child. She would sometimes encourage a period of intensive therapy for the sufferer to try to connect with events or conditions that had "caused" the depression. Other times she would simply state that her own depressions usually passed with time. Lea also had periods of hypo-mania during which she would feel elation, enormous energy and confidence, and periods of sleeplessness. It was possibly during these times that she would take on larger and larger loads which, once the phase passed, would leave her feeling overwhelmed and exhausted. People close to Lea were aware of her cycles from early days. She would speak of going up into a manic phase. The euphoria, the ascending were dramatic and exciting, but before long they would push her over the edge. When she went to North Carolina in 1968 for treatment for diabetes, the cycles were coming more to the fore. Her pattern of dealing with their effects was to hide from them by focusing on her physical problems. But the condition became more and more obvious as she got older.

Without the impact of her mental health and psychological difficulties, Lea might have been more able to deal with her diabetes in a consistent and grounded fashion. Glenda, who travelled with her from the late 1960s said that,

> "In North Carolina Lea learned a lot about Type-II diabetes. At Duke University, they were at the forefront of work with that illness. She knew what it was and what to do about it, but she didn't do it. I know others who are doing well on the regime -- basically just diet and exercise. But Lea had a lot of food compulsions. She could have been quite well if she had followed their directions. But instead she chased one fad after another. She'd believe the most god-awful ridiculous things. It was saviour-hunting rather than simply getting down to taking proper care of herself. I think I've met most of the quacks in the western world."

Throughout the 1970s, Lea followed a succession of programs in the name of health which at root were a way of distracting herself from issues that she was not prepared or able to deal with. Macrobiotics and fasting would alternate with periods of bingeing. Nutritionists and healers of many stripes would be consulted, and their ideas incorporated into her practices and those of the people who most closely followed her. In the process, Lea undermined her own health and compromised that of others.

The Learning Groups

Lea with a learning group in the large group room at the Willow

There is much to be said about the learning groups that Lea founded after the original Hypnotherapy Group, about their orientations, processes, and outcomes. That first group was a site wherein Lea worked long and hard at the actual business of psychotherapy, teaching her students by doing. None of the subsequent groups was particularly successful. Some participants did become therapists for the long haul, but significantly fewer with each succeeding "generation" of learners. After Hypno I there was Hypno II, incorporated into the seminar after a year, then CAG, a short-lived Hypno III group (disbanded because of the amount of questioning and disagreement with Lea's ideas), the Brunswick learners, Gemini I and

II, and in 1979, another short-lived group, the New Learners. Why did Lea continue to found these groups?

When she returned from North Carolina, Lea had essentially surrendered her practice to the therapists who had taken over in her absence. This work had been her source of income. Around that time, the finances of what was now called Therafields became administered centrally. Therapists were paid a salary based on the size of their practices. Lea needed a job. Having more and more learners provided a focus for her and a raison d'etre. She was Teacher, Supervisor, and Ultimate Leader. The groups also provided an impetus for Therafields itself. Pairs of neophytes were turned loose on the constant stream of people coming for therapy in the early 1970s. Other than the first wave of therapists from the Hypnotherapy group, learners did not receive remuneration for their work. Rather, all revenue generated by them went into the general coffers to pay for the administration, the farm, the on-going construction projects promoted by Visvaldis, and his and Lea's salaries.

Lea's relationship with those of us in the Character Analysis Group was a peculiar one. We would meet for marathon sessions that were to assist us in becoming better therapists. In the sessions Lea posed, and was positioned by us, as the Great Teacher, but in truth by the early to mid-1970s she did not have a great deal to teach. If she was honestly working through her own problems, she might have had something more interesting to impart. In fact, she was well past her peak as a therapist and as a teacher and was now coasting along on an image of herself built up in the mid-1960s, later elaborated by the trappings of the life-style that Visvaldis encouraged and that we built for her.

In group sessions if she didn't have a recent enthusiasm with which to spur conversation, Lea would invite people to ask her questions. The idea was quite explicitly articulated that we collectively had all the knowledge currently available to humanity to deal with any psychological problems. By the mid-1970s Lea was actively discouraging people from pursuing any kind of learning from sources outside of Therafields. To one woman she asked, "Why would you want to take those summer courses at the university when you could spend the summer working up here at the farm?" or to another, "Why would you want to have friends outside of Therafields? People outside of our community have nothing to offer me!"

When John M pursued a connection with the people at Findhorn in Scotland, Lea was so opposed that eventually he and his partner left behind their very long relationship with her and with Therafields. Jim Healy arranged to study body work with Gerda Boyson in England. Lea attacked him openly in groups, trying to convince him that he was deluded to think that he had anything to learn from Gerda. He went anyway and later studied as well at the Jungian Institute in Switzerland.

Moreover, Lea progressively developed an anti-intellectual bias. No longer was there an encouragement to read current writers. If, as she stated, we collectively had all pertinent knowledge needed to deal with psychological difficulties, it appeared more and more that that knowledge was essentially to be revealed by Lea herself. In a seminar meeting someone suggested that different members could study some of the more important psychotherapists and then teach them to the whole of the group. He mentioned that one of the women present could, for example, teach the Freudian canon, as she had just completed a PhD degree focused on his work. Lea looked witheringly at the woman singled out, saying, "What could you possibly have to teach me?". End of discussion.

Looking back on some of the learning groups and seminars, it would be almost amusing to think of the directions taken, were it not for the fact that we so-called learners were putting a great deal of time, energy, and money into the process and yet learning little. The things that Lea incessantly talked about through the early 1970s were: the paranee/paranoid issue; the emotional plague; cyclothymic versus schizoid personality types; fasting and related health issues; the importance of viewing Therafields as a working i.e., building community; and increasingly, Visvaldis' fantasized Environmental Centre. These all flowed from her own unresolved issues, her family problems, and the needs of Visvaldis.

The "paranee/paranoid" construction was Lea's own. She coupled it with Reich's idea of "the emotional plague," taken initially from the last chapter of his book, *Character Analysis*. Reich spoke of "the emotional plague" suffered by an individual, not as inner malevolence, or moral degeneracy, but as a condition imposed upon him or her from infancy, as natural expressions of genital sexuality were suppressed. His mission was to educate people about healthy sexuality for themselves, and importantly, for their children. Reich passionately condemned the way that each generation passed on its own thwarted sexuality to the one coming after, but his analysis did not condemn the individual so afflicted.

This was not Lea's understanding and use of Reich's phrase. From her earliest reading of his books, she blended some of his ideas with Freudian and Kleinian approaches, brewing interpretations that related to issues with which she herself was dealing. The emotional plague, the "devouring" impulses of the infant, and the "destruction of the matrix," were all grist to her theoretical mill. As early as 1967, Lea was admonishing workers at the farm that carelessness with her furniture was an indication of hatred of the matrix, a desire to destroy the mother – not said, but implied -- herself. Over the next years, she continually elaborated her ideas about the emotional plague found in relationships between what she called, "the paranoid and the paranee," The "paranoid" was typecast as a devourer – one who sucked the life essence of his or her victim "paranee."

Depending upon the actual person being designated paranoid, judgments about them varied. In the summer of 1969 when Josie was separating from her first husband, Tom, and Lea had moved away from Harry and into her relationship with Visvaldis, the two women gave angry examples in groups about their husbands' foibles. The men's behaviours, narrowness, and negativity were trotted forth to demonstrate how the women had been kept from having full lives. Only by moving away from their partners had they been free to live their own "glorious lives" to the full. These "paranoids" were not viewed as evil, however, as were some in later years. They were simply described as rather pathetic creatures, ruled internally by unacknowledged fear and their need to latch onto another for emotional substance and security.

Lea morphed Reich's phrase "emotional plague," from a physical condition of constriction, protecting a person from painful or frightening emotions, to a characterological condition of hatred and evil. The "paranoid" became the carrier and spreader of the emotional plague. In her work with individuals around 1969-70 Lea often put stress upon perceived components of paranoia in the client's partner, counselling separation as the best antidote. Several, especially men, close to her, did separate at least temporarily from their partners.

Other important conceptual references that Lea took from Reich were embodied in his texts *The Murder of Christ* and *Listen Little Man*. These books were sold at the farm and in the main office on Dupont Street, and were referred to often by Lea in groups as important for the understanding of human behaviour. As Lea had become more defended and less secure, she had gathered about herself those upon whom she could utterly depend: Rob, Barry, Visvaldis, the women who in various ways took care of her, and others from whom she extracted "loyalty" sometimes based on her conviction, and theirs, that she had "saved their lives." This group shifted, growing and diminishing over the years, but always being her bulwark against the threatening "other," those whom she came to fear could destroy her and her work. In Reich's texts she found the language to articulate this position.

The Murder of Christ was written by Reich as an expression of his view of the problems experienced in all millennia by people like himself who strove to do good. According to Reich, the main dividing line between people was those who are genital in character and those who are not. The distinction is clearly pejorative: genital character, good – like Christ and God, at one with nature; non-genital character, bad – connected with evil and the devil and liable to attack and murder the Christ figure. In this work Reich clearly identifies himself with Christ and the genital character. Those who disagree with him are the murderers, though they may pose as Christ's admirers.

> "They love Jesus because he is what they are not and what they cannot ever be. They try to drink his strength and simplicity and spontaneous beauty into themselves. But they do not succeed. They cannot be like Christ nor take him in ...(Christ) does not retain and hold onto his strength. He gives it out abundantly, never giving a thought to whether or not he would get richer or poorer by giving.... The (non-genital characters) do not know what he is talking about. To them, giving away things means getting poorer. Taking is the same as getting strength, filling up an emptiness, getting over a yawning gap within oneself. They can only take, they cannot give. They shut up many a giver, drive into solitude many a loving soul." (pp. 31-2)

Reich derived this analysis from his therapeutic work:

"We know from character-analytic explorations of man's depth structure that it is his basic genital disturbance, his orgiastic impotence, which keeps him confined. It is, therefore, quite consistent that he will persecute and punish nothing more severely, that he will hate nothing more abundantly than the graceful appearance of orgiastic potency, i.e., the Life of Christ, i.e., his own cosmic origin and present potentiality."

The central focus of Reich's book is on a divide written in black and white between those who are good, loving, and givers of life, and those who are disturbed, takers and users, filled with hatred of the good. Lea identified with Reich and with his description of the genital character, the Christ figure. By the summer of 1969 she was speaking of devourers and had developed her theory of the "paranee/paranoid." These categories closely resemble Reich's "Little Man" and his "Christ figure." The language and approach contrasted markedly with Lea's earlier work in psychotherapy and her relations with clients and her groups. Her version of "Love the sinner but hate the sin," which had been "Love the troubled person but go toward the disturbance that is limiting him or her," now became "the disturbance itself is evil and the carrier of the disturbance is suspect and a potential danger."

The Murder of Christ had been published by the trustees of Reich's Infant Trust Fund in 1952. Their introduction to the book states that the problems that Reich outlines in his book are real, but that Reich's solutions in it are "immature, emotionally blurred, insufficient or lacking completeness." They further state that they decided to publish the book simply as an historical document. This introduction was not included in the newer copies sold at the farm.

Throughout the early 1970s, Lea would use Reich's ideas and her own spin on them centrally in her role as a teacher. On a marathon in early 1974 with her two Gemini groups, Lea opened by suggesting that the focus of their weekend meetings be on the emotional plague and on paranoid/paranee relationships. Lea's general method of proceeding while teaching, was to have people ask questions. She believed that when people ask questions or make comments, they reveal what they understand or what they are confused about. She believed that when someone lectures, listeners take it in in their own fashion, not necessarily in the way intended by the speaker. With the Q&A format, more could be seen about the individual speaking and about any confusions or distortions that he or she carried. From records taken, I can give some examples of questions and answers given on this marathon:

Who lives longest in a paranoid/paranee marriage?

Lea: almost always the paranee dies first. In most of these kinds of marriages, the paranee is quite literally eaten up by the paranoia. In most cases though, if the paranee finds another, a lover or something, very often that is helpful.

What is the attraction for the paranee to the paranoid?

Lea: usually the paranee is quite a strong person and will have a lot of parenting instincts; very often he is sorry for the poor little paranoid. But also, the paranoid can have a great deal of personal charm to draw the paranee in: the typical spider. He has the kind of charm that a paranee is a sucker for. Once the paranoid has the paranee, he can be in a strong position, especially once there are kids. He can take his venom out on them, or he can turn them against his partner. In my opinion, the basis of paranoia is cannibalism. The paranoiac is usually a very cannibalistic person.

What makes a person paranoid?

Lea: paranoia is basically an outgrowth of fear, though it could be any of a thousand things that caused a person to become paranoid. Paranoia is the emotional plague: the person prefers death to life, unhappiness to joy; he cannot do creative work because he is blocked; he can't enjoy his children because he is afraid of the life within them; he's afraid of his own children growing larger because he feels very small. What is that but the plague? It does spread like the plague. It spreads in families, it spreads from generation to generation. It's like a malicious weed that grows up and the moment your back is turned, it will smother living and vital work.

Can two paranoids be partnered?

Lea: A relationship between two paranoids is hell on earth; it is the marriage of two children. Their children are almost always psychotic, or they will die in infancy. I know of a girl of nine whose parents are both paranoid: the girl is riddled with cancer.

In Therafields certain people have a lot of the emotional plague. Can they spread it around?

Lea: Yes. Someone who is doing well in his therapy, can be with a person who starts telling him things negative about Therafields. (The person) might refute them at the time, but it will play on his mind; it'll torture him. When he goes to his session, he'll be polluted. He won't be able to work on his own inner problems; he'll be working on this surface thing. This is object illness. He'll be working on the illness of the other who dropped it on him. But that's not as serious as giving that to a child in his formative years.

How do you work with a paranoid and with a paranee?

Lea: With the paranoid, you must let him be as un-frightened as possible. But you can't be terribly sweet with him; he will see through that and hate you. He will think that you are afraid of treading on his toes. Being straightforward is the best. With the paranee: it's hard to do much for her if the paranoid is not involved (in the therapy work). I have worked with some who were able to leave their relationship. They outgrow it; are freed of it. The paranee has much more energy; the paranoid less because his creativity is blocked. The classical idea of the paranoid is that he thinks that someone is always after him. That's only one part of the picture; the area of cannibalism in the paranoid is likely the last part to be given up. When the paranoid first is involved with the paranee, he can go through a creative period: his energy can rise, and he will seem fascinating and attractive; he'll eventually draw the victim in. Once the victim is in his clutches, he surrounds the victim completely. He tries to draw the victim from her friends and family. Then he will try to interfere with the victim's creativity.

In the above answer Lea seems to be speaking specifically about her own situation with her husband Harry, for whom she blamed the problems in her marriage and family.

In these settings, Lea would acknowledge that everyone has a certain amount of paranoia and that not all relationships followed the patterns laid down by a paranoid/paranee duality. These were to be viewed as exceptional, cases that one would see as a therapist. There were several difficulties with this disclaimer, however. Separate from any broader set of teachings, this typology loomed large for her students. Though she was speaking with a "learning" group, the group had no formal instructions or texts that could situate these ideas within other frameworks of pathology and mental health. The "medical student syndrome" was in full operation: am I or is the person sitting here with me a paranoid or a paranee? Moreover, as Lea's interest, passion, and eloquence about these ideas sprang from her own justifications for leaving her marriage to Harry and for Visvaldis leaving his to Mildred, she found the syndrome of the paranoid/paranee relationship wherever she looked.

When one of the group members on this marathon (I will call him George) was seen to be upset, she initiated a focus on his relationship with his girlfriend. She knew that George had been profoundly tied to his mother, a relationship that caused him to be ambivalent toward women. As George drew closer to a woman who attracted him, he would experience fear and a sense of being smothered. He loved his girlfriend but felt conflicted about being close to her.

Lea did not work with his problems. Rather she asked people present to talk about the woman with whom he was involved. Many spoke of her as a strong and good person, but Lea was more interested in comments made that might reveal weakness. She said that when George had been in Florida, people there had spoken well of the young woman. But she was suspicious. "What is she doing in therapy if she is so strong and wholesome?" she thought. Lea spoke of a time that she had done some work with the young woman in a group.

> "When I worked with her, I was working with pure evil. There was nothing else there, it seemed. She'd come forth with some sweet sickly things, but there was so much evil there, there was no way of reaching it. Where are all these false notions about her coming from? I want to look at the truth of this; you people joined a conspiracy."

A member of the group said, "I'm confused because to me she is a creative person. It's not like she waits for him for every move she makes. She takes initiative on her own." Lea replied, "I find myself getting very irritated with this. It's not rigid. Supposing she did not have a victim, would she be as creative? There are lots of people who can only be creative when they have a victim."

This "work" on the marathon destroyed George's relationship. His tie to Lea was such that he could not go against her. When with his girlfriend, his already problematical connection with her, coupled with Lea's words, overwhelmed the good things that they had had together. Into the present, George regrets his inability to remain faithful to this woman in the face of Lea's condemnation. A coda to this little story: George was invited down to Florida not too much later where he was 'encouraged' into a relationship with one of Lea's proteges, a young woman who longed for a mate and children.

Another session of that marathon began with a general talk about the importance of being aware and active when one sees reprehensible things, for example, parents being unkind or abusive with children. The conversation was interrupted by a woman who wanted Lea to know about the precarious situation of one of the group members, whom I will call Gwen. Gwen had moved into a house group two months earlier and was now also a member of the Gemini group. Gwen was subject to intense asthmatic episodes, some of which had happened since she had moved into the house group. During an attack she was liable to pass out and she had been taken to the hospital more than once. At that moment, she was recovering in another room from such an attack. A few people were with her.

People from Gwen's house group said that when she was having an attack, her therapists were sometimes called. They would come over and talk with her; sometimes she would get a massage and would feel better. Lea, who had never worked with Gwen, said, "She has probably somatized her desire for love. Being ill draws caring and sympathy. It sets up a pattern of behaviour as she gets attention." Gwen's friend from the house group said that recent talk in group sessions about paranoia and devouring had confused Gwen as she now believed that her attacks were a decision she was making in order to draw people in, to devour them.

Lea asked,

> "I wonder if she is ready for a learning group; I'm doubtful. She is years away from being ready to work with people. She'll have to be completely cleansed from the tendency to fall into illnesses before she would be allowed to work. If she's going to become physically ill, I don't want her in one of my learning groups. I don't see the point of it. She should be taken home."

Another group member said,

> "I see what you mean Lea, that this is her way of getting attention on the one hand; on the other hand, when she has an attack, it's terribly confused; she doesn't know

whether she's coming or going; she's really both ways in moments of alarm. She feels really guilty about all of this – that she's not getting out her real feelings to be able to move on from it."

Another member put in, "Maybe this is callous, but people make their own decisions." Lea's son Rob then said, "This is serious business, like what happened to Karl (a man who died after a long fast). It feels like the great struggle of life and death. It feels in a way like it is being held over the group." Lea responded, "Exactly; it's as though the whole group is paying the price for this." She asked the group members to say what they knew about Gwen's family background. It was reported that "Her mother was very devouring; her father was a doctor. He had a serious heart attack and later developed Parkinson's and died about ten years ago. Gwen's mother had died during an asthmatic attack which makes Gwen's episodes that much more frightening for her." Lea commented, "It seems the parents were two children -- that has a terrible effect on their offspring."

Another member of the group said,

"Gwen's attacks are an acting out of anger. There are areas of real primitive rage in people that can kill you. With Gwen, rather than feel her incredible anger, she goes into an asthmatic attack. If she doesn't feel the anger, then everyone else does."

Lea responded,

"We have all been crippled and entangled by this talk. People who suffer from psychosomatic illnesses should be given good treatment and cared for. But they get something out of being ill. I think that this girl's illness is her entire life. I don't believe there is very much more in her life. Is there anything?"

Her friend said that she paints portraits, sings in the choir and writes poetry. Lea had no comment.

After a break, a doctor who was a group member explained the physiology of asthma. "Not everyone uses it psychologically," he said. Lea agreed but said,

> "I believe it was this girl's first defence against being a frustrated infant. Looking at her face and her body you can see her as a frustrated infant. She needs to go into the agonizing feelings that she had before she jumped into the asthma."

Lea suggested that people find other things in Gwen that attract them – not the illness; she also suggested that she go on a grape diet to cleanse her body.

Gwen was driven downtown by one of the people who had come up for the day to work on construction. None of her housemates accompanied her as Lea thought that the marathon ought not to be further disrupted. Gwen died a few months later during one of her asthma attacks.

This episode illustrates Lea's contention that illness is traceable to psychological disorders, a not uncommon New Age perspective of the period, certainly underscored by Reich's later writings, for example, in *The Cancer Biopathy* published posthumously in 1973. The interaction of the group also shows their inability/unwillingness to strongly stand up for Gwen in her distress or to challenge Lea's superficial analysis and conclusions about her situation. Even by the late 1960s Lea was essentially unassailable in any group context. She had always her 'assistants' with her to help counter any negative thought or argument. In this context Rob was the person confirming the direction of her thinking. Any person challenging Lea would be pushed back, confronted, and humiliated. Others would not speak on the challenger's behalf, fearing a similar fate. More seriously though was the effect this silencing had upon members of the community – causing many to call into question their own responses, thinking that Lea and her helpers must be right and they themselves deluded. It was in this manner that from the late 1960s, elements that can only be called cultic took root within the Therafields landscape. There were others who maintained considerably more skeptical positions vis-a-vis Lea and some of her ideas. But until the late 1970s there was never any united push-back, and then it only coalesced around issues related to finances.

Regarding Homosexuality

The difficult earlier situation to which Rob had alluded during this group session referred to the death a year or so earlier of Karl Lopez, another of Lea's "learners." Lea was experimenting with long fasts not just to reduce weight but likely also as a way of distracting herself from problems she could not deal with both within herself and within her immediate family. Lea could have stabilized her weight and her blood sugar levels by adhering to the regular diet and exercise regime that the doctors at Duke University had prescribed for her. Instead she continually oscillated between over-eating and a series of fad diets. From at least this period she was also making use of 'diet' pills that would reduce hunger but also give her an energy boost at times that she needed it. She would consult with various interested persons both within and outside the Therafields community and would periodically strike off in some new and radical departure. Others would become swept up in her enthusiasms. Karl was one of those who went along with the idea of a lengthy fast as a vehicle for approaching unresolved personal difficulties. Aside from whatever early, familial baggage he might have been carrying, Karl's big issue within the Therafields community lay in the fact that he was homosexual in the period well before societal acceptance had been gained for his sexual orientation.

Lea's own views about homosexuality were strangely ambivalent. She read and recommended Edmund Bergler's 1956 book, *Homosexuality: Disease or Way of Life*, in which Bergler argued that homosexuality was a curable disease. The thrust of her attitude, and that of those whom she trained in her early learning groups, adhered to Bergler's view. People coming into therapy with an already existing homosexual or lesbian relationship, quickly found themselves separated from their partners.

They would be given different therapists, different standard and house groups. Generally, they would be given the message that continuance of the relationship was a destructive act – often with the blame placed on one of the partners as the active – i.e., "perpetrating" agent of the other's "victimhood." The goal was to "cure" the homosexual, to turn him or her into a heterosexual, or at least an inactive sexual person. As the community grew and Lea's influence was less personal in these situations, attitudes against homosexuality and homosexuals themselves became standard practice. People like Karl suffered terribly.

When Lea spoke of homosexuality in my early group around 1966-7, she appeared to be trying to understand how this orientation had come about. She would, for example, compare having an attraction to someone of one's own gender and becoming sexually involved with that person, as similar to the difference between having a fantasy of being violent toward another, and actually being violent. The individual was crossing a line into behaviour that could only be viewed as either psychopathic or psychotic. She did not spell out this analogy in accusatory ways, because she cared for the people who were stimulating her reflections. Still, for young and impressionable learners like myself, the implied message was that homosexual activity indicated seriously disturbed behaviour.

Later, when Lea no longer worked directly with individuals as in earlier days, she would include in her "theoretical considerations," conclusions about homosexuals and homosexuality. On the Gemini marathon written of above, Lea made the statement that homosexual partnerships were usually ghastly connections between two paranoids, certain to destroy one another. She mentioned Bergler in this context, saying though she respected his work, that he connected everything related to homosexuality to masochism, and that his approach was too narrow. She herself would see homosexuals as very good people with much to contribute. It was a profoundly double message to those of our community dealing with social opprobrium both outside and within the group to which they had come for help. You are a good person but if you are an active homosexual – not so good. People like Karl and others were given intensive therapy with the purpose of "curing" them. If they attempted a heterosexual alliance they were deemed particularly wonderful and their therapy a success.

There was a certain threat or dread associated with the idea of homosexuality in the community in the late 1960s and 1970s. Gus, one of Lea's early clients and a member of the first learning group, would speak of it in terms perhaps learned in his native Newfoundland. It became known jokingly as "dat der queerness," or "dat der" for short. Many references were made both seriously and in fun about emotional connections between men or between women that smacked of this element. If it was spoken of seriously, the intent was to call attention to certain destructive components in the relationship; if in fun, it was used as a tease. For gay or lesbian people who entered therapy because of the same kinds of confusions and unhappiness that brought any of us to seek help, it was no laughing matter. Their sexual orientation was viewed as a central problem that had to be corrected if their therapy was to be successful.

The following recollections are those of a man whose therapy and life were blighted by this approach:

"When I look back on my therapy the thing I am most bitter about is the amount of homophobia that I suffered – starting with Lea. She had an investment in turning everyone out straight, with the men adoring her. All the feelings of self-loathing that a gay person experiences in this culture anyway were greatly amplified there. It was so wrong. The main thing I have had to deal with since leaving Therafields has been deprogramming myself from the homophobia that was inflicted upon me. My therapist spent a lot of time trying to "cure" me of homosexuality. I spent 12 years trying. It was very painful, truly horrible. Gay people in Therafields took an incredible amount of bashing. Lea would talk about homosexuality as being the same formation within a person as paedophilia."

I know none of the particulars of Karl's journey before the beginning of his long fast, though others of his acquaintance know how he struggled with being homosexual within the Therafields context. He was not successfully "cured." He went on the fast undoubtedly as another person embracing with Lea a radical path to health. Others on the fast came off it at various stages, but Karl persisted. Toward the end he was bedridden at the house group residence where he lived. I believe that he had fasted close to 60 days by that point. People in his house group were left to care for him though none had any medical training or understanding of what was happening to Karl's body. Stan B, a GP, was not his doctor, but would be asked by Lea to keep an eye on people who were doing the fast. At the time Stan was more or less going along with Lea's fasting adventures. After a couple of days with Karl passing in and out of a semi-comatose state, he died.

Karl's death resounded throughout Therafields like a bomb going off. How could this have happened? The people with whom he lived and his friends were profoundly traumatized by the event. An inquest was held but no accountability was assigned. His death was attributed to his own decision to continue the fasting process regardless of the entreaties of friends and housemates to terminate it. It was viewed by most who knew him as a suicide, gradually embarked upon as the fast entered more precarious stages. Karl was not, and was not going to be, a "successfully cured" homosexual.

At a group held at the Willow shortly after Karl's death, Lea raged on about it. She was furious with him for having given up his life rather than continuing as did she to battle with her problems. I remember being shocked at her attitude toward a man who had just died, someone for whom she had presumably cared. Lea took his death personally, saying in essence to Karl, "How could you do this to me? How could you bring me and Therafields into a public forum of inquiry?" Obviously, others close to Lea adopted her feelings as there was never any open conversation within groups about the methodology of extensive fasting or of Lea's own responsibility in advocating a technique rife with destructive possibilities. Lea could not take responsibility, certainly not publicly, for the outcomes in which she had a hand. When Rob said in the Gemini marathon that he had a feeling in the group of it being taken over by Gwen's asthmatic attack, and that it reminded him of what had happened earlier with Karl, he was reflecting his mother's conclusion that Karl had destructively impacted Therafields by his decision to die as a result of his long fast.

Other 'Health' interventions and 'Teachings'

A year or so after the Gemini marathon described above, Lea became involved in the "care" of a young woman who had developed a severe abdominal illness. Joyce (a pseudonym) had been struggling with a form of irritable bowel syndrome. Lea became convinced that the problem was a stomach ulcer caused by some unrevealed area of guilt. Joyce was moved into a Toronto apartment of another Therafields therapist that adjoined Lea's own. For a few days Joyce was put under the care of a succession of women from the CAG group, none of whom had any medical training. Lea would attend periodically to talk with Joyce about her unresolved issues though Joyce's condition continued to worsen. Stan, the GP who had been somewhat involved with Karl, was called in to see her. He recognized at once that she was in a critical state, likely from the loss of electrolytes, and moved quickly to have her admitted to hospital. The admitting doctor was furious with the women who accompanied her to the hospital, saying that if she had not been brought in then, she would have died. Joyce was given intravenous and steroids. Her condition improved rapidly.

There were other examples of Lea's interference in health issues. I am writing only about ones of which I have some knowledge, and I was by no means a part of Lea's inner circle. In 1976 a four-month-old baby of one of the seminar women was having an allergic reaction of some nature to the formula she was receiving. She was referred to a naturopathic doctor whom Lea was seeing. This professional – I don't know his actual qualifications – put the baby on a liquid diet of vegetables. The mother, already insecure in her position with the child, acquiesced. Several days later the baby swooned and slipped into unconsciousness, luckily when not alone. Her mother wasted no time being driven to Sick Children's Hospital. In the emergency room, an admitting nurse took the baby and literally ran with her to an examining doctor. As luck would have it, one intern in attendance recognized the symptoms as a toxic reaction to the vegetable juices the child was being fed and an antidote was immediately given. The baby survived and is now a healthy mother with children of her own. The "doctor" who had prescribed the vegetable juices was denounced by the medical team at Sick Kids'. He left Canada soon afterwards. Lea and her family were angry with the mother for having given the hospital contact information of the man when asked. Lea at no time referred to or took responsibility for this episode which might have ended in the death of that beautiful child.

In 1973 or 1974 Lea began to talk in marathon groups about two personality types: the cyclothymic and the schizoid. Here was a new framework on which to judge or be judged. (There is an old joke that goes like this: There are two kinds of people in the world -- those who categorize everyone into two groups, and those who don't). There was endless discussion about this new typology, the characteristics of each 'personality,' and which it was more desirable to be. It seemed that being cyclothymic gave one a leg up on the schizoid type. Lea identified herself as cyclothymic, an expansive and creative personality. The poor little schizoid, by comparison, was a plodder, a boring but diligent person who could be depended upon to complete the large tasks envisioned by his or her cyclothymic counterpart Just as one did not want to be labelled a paranoid, the idea of being schizoid was dreadful. There wasn't any sense of humour about these designations either. Lea was trying to understand her own powerful mood swings, undoubtedly growing stronger as the decade of the 1970s progressed. In the process, however, many others designated schizoid felt scourged by the sense of being diminished and thus not respected or valued. Like the earlier paranoid/paranee dichotomy, the 'personality types' were sprung upon Lea's learners without any broader context of normal and abnormal psychology. There it was – two possibilities. Take your choice.

One other arena for periodic, though quite unproductive, contemplation was that of sexuality. In the early days Lea would sometimes come into a group and say, "Let's talk about sex." "Oh yes," a dozen lips would sigh. Many in Lea's original groups were either former religious or had backgrounds rife with sexual repression. Unfortunately, there was no one in the groups free enough sexually to actually broach a discussion that would be helpful: not the group members and not Lea herself. I was one of the seriously uninitiated who would have welcomed an adult conversation like those embarked upon by sexual counsellors of a later era. But in the groups, a long, somewhat embarrassed, silence would follow the initial foray. There might be a few jokes. I remember one former priest saying that he had begun "taking his sexuality into his own hands." Lots of guffaws.

At the farm in its first year, Lea invited the women who were present there one weekend to meet with her in the farmhouse for a talk. In this context she tried to promote a conversation about sex. Little was forthcoming though the atmosphere was friendly and warm. Lea made an attempt by speaking about oral sex. She asked one of the more mature women there, a woman maybe five or ten years older than myself, a woman whom Lea knew to have had several relationships, if she liked oral sex. The woman was embarrassed but struggled to be helpful, saying that she had never found it particularly pleasurable. Lea said that that had been her experience as well. This little snippet of conversation lodged in my brain. I'm not sure that I really even understood the act they were dismissing. At least ten years later the topic came up once again in a meeting of the combined seminar group (Hypno 1 and CAG) at the Willow. By then Lea's pondering of the phenomena of oral sex had moved from, "I don't get much from it." to, "This is an infantile form of sexuality, a symptom of serious personality disintegration." A woman who had clearly spoken to Lea earlier (perhaps on being directly asked) about her partner's desire for oral sex, was called upon to discuss the issue to the detriment of her partner, not a seminar member but well-known to all present. It was an embarrassing colloquy, not just for this woman, but undoubtedly for most of us present, though no one endeavoured to educate Lea about the joys of sexual freedom.

Another issue about intimacy was also on Lea's agenda at this period: She would make statements about the importance of couples having separate places to sleep on those nights that they did not plan to have sexual relations. I remember clearly sitting on a bench close to the steps leading up from the Willow's group room, or on the steps themselves, hearing Lea speak of these concerns. None of those conversations had much relevance for me. I neither embraced nor dismissed the things of which she spoke. I kept off to one side, listening, making no judgments, but essentially going my own way with respect to my growing sense of adult sexuality. It seems to me that few people entered into these topics with enthusiasm. Perhaps most others kept their own reservations to themselves. As in many other areas that she would highlight, I believe that Lea often spoke out of reflections she was making that referred to her own life at the time.

During the period of 1967 to the late 1970s there was, however, one significant phase of teaching. On the seminar's summer marathon of 1973 Lea introduced a new form of work with which she had been experimenting, likely with a few people with whom she still did some psychotherapy. The idea most certainly came from the then current book by Janov, *The Primal Scream*, though Lea did not acknowledge this source. She attributed it rather to Freud's writings about "abreaction," a healing release of affect connected with early trauma and held repressed in the unconscious, or, as Reich would have it, in the body. Lea demonstrated this work by asking one of her retinue to allow her to show the group the therapy that she was doing privately with her. The woman lay down on cushions near Lea, who, using her hypnosis technique, placed her in a state of relaxation. Then Lea began to speak to the woman very directly, stimulating painful memories and feelings. I don't remember the exact words that she used but they could have been something like, "No, mommy doesn't love you. You're all alone. There's no one here for you." Whatever the message was, it was very explicit and related to the woman's early experience. She immediately reacted to Lea's words, becoming upset and crying in obvious pain. It was not an act. One could feel the power of the work that was being done.

During the rest of that marathon we used this method of working, always in the group setting. The group would split roughly in half – one half to be worked with and the other half as partners, to assist them in the work. Lea, or someone else, would take five minutes or so to induce relaxation. Then each partner would begin to make direct statements to the person being worked with, often like the words that Lea used in her demonstration. The statements would be tailored to the individual working and what was known about his or her early history. The results were quite spectacular. Many of us connected with and released pent up emotions, the strength of which surprised and exhilarated us. The work released for me and for others a great deal of energy and hope for new and lively possibilities. I equally liked working with others and being worked with. It was dynamic and it showed immediate results for anyone able to surrender herself to it. The several years of body work that I had done gave me a good preparation for it and I wasn't afraid.

When we returned to the city, this work continued. Abreactive groups were set up as a regular adjunct to therapy. Only people in learning groups partook of this work as it was deemed experimental. The groups took place in the large second-floor room at 316 Dupont in the early mornings, 7-8AM, I believe. I would be up by 6:30 three mornings a week to participate. One morning was for the seminar group where I would work and be worked with. The other two mornings were for other learning groups led by Adam. I asked him if I could come along to help, as I was very interested in this aspect of therapy. Each of those mornings I would work with people and sometimes would give the preliminary relaxation. This involvement continued my developing confidence as a worker and increased my sense of commitment and connection as a learner. On a personal level, most of what I felt when being worked with, related to the fear and anger that I had contained in my body from being hit as a child, even up to a year or so before I left home at 19. Until that period, my unspoken assumption had been that all kids were hit a lot, that it was just a fact of life and not a big deal. But as I cried and raged, I began to more deeply realize the scarring effect these experiences had had on me. I had been hurt, humiliated, betrayed, violated, and made to feel very badly about myself. My parents undoubtedly had received similar treatment when they were children and were passing on what they had experienced when consumed by their own moments of frustration. However, I was still a long way from feeling forgiveness or understanding of them.

Families and Children

As the number of people asking for therapy grew, among them were parents of children struggling with their family's problems. The answer to the needs of almost anyone coming along at that point was to put them into a house group, to surround them with others for support. By early 1970 several families had moved into Therafields' houses on Kendal and Brunswick Avenues. A number of the houses backed onto one another. Once fences were removed, a large open space became available for children's activities and for easy communal connections. Each family lived together with single persons who were interested in being involved with the children. Unfortunately, there wasn't enough good judgment shown about who would and who would not be ready for such an experience, who would and who would not be able to handle it in a manner conducive to good outcomes for themselves and those with whom they lived. House group and milieu life was simply not a productive experience for some people. They tended either to act out in ways that could not then be given proper boundaries, or, they were so overwhelmed by the emotional life of the group that they could not access their own thoughts or feelings. As this was true of individuals, so it was true with families. Some undoubtedly benefited from the practical help and support of the members of their milieu or of those living with them. Others did not.

In the fall of 1970 Lea's newest learning group formed a "milieu" in the group of houses in that area, becoming known as the Brunswick Learning Group. Many of the original members already lived within the complex; others then moved in or were associated in various ways from that time. All living there, as many as 40 people, began to have house groups together. The impetus for the development of house groups formed around individual families would have come from Lea. No initiatives were begun without her spear-heading energy and interest. But the project was too broad, too ambitious given the level of understanding and therapeutic skills available. Lea considered herself to be a specialist with children and families though this was not true. She had been unable to resolve her own troubles with respect to her family of origin and with her own family. ML, who had been close to Lea through most of the 1960s and 1970s said,

> "Earlier she was helping people, but then her own disturbance came to the surface. To continue to help people, she had to look into herself and do her own work. Instead she took on more and more distractions."

Taking on the enormous job of working with and supervising the care and mental health of such a huge and complex milieu was one more of the "distractions" that Lea embraced as she moved away from going deeper personally or with her original clients. Working with the families stirred even more of her own troubles, making objectivity impossible.

Meg recalled,

> "Pressure from her work with the families on Brunswick brought up a lot of her own personal difficulties, reminding her of bad times in her own early years. During a marathon in the city with the Brunswick group, Lea called me during a lunch break and asked me to come and give her a massage. When I saw her, I was appalled because she was in no shape to be working with anyone. She was a woman working in a large emotional pressure cooker and she had to deal with issues very like her own with these families. I remember thinking that she was so personally involved in what was happening with them that she had entirely lost objectivity. I asked her to talk to me about what she was experiencing, but she didn't really do so."

Lea had presented her own family of origin and her relationships with her children in glowing terms and she had to maintain that fiction, even to herself. She believed that her instincts were right and were to be followed with respect to the needs of children and their parents. But in fact, she sometimes acted in ways that had the effect of significantly damaging those whom she wished to help. Her certainty about decisions swayed others and brought them along with her in arrangements which interfered badly with some of the families.

Like the situation with Margaret and Lisa recounted earlier, if in a family of the milieu the mother seemed not "up to" the job of caring for and protecting her children, Lea's solution would be cavalier. Give the child to another woman who could manage. During the life of the Brunswick milieu, several children were removed from their mothers and placed in other situations. In one case, the mother, deemed emotionally insufficient, was encouraged to leave; the father found other women within the group to help him with his children. Another father had left his wife and children around 1969 under the influence of talk about paranoid partners. A few years later, his wife, who was caring for their three children, was judged a poor mother by her therapist (significantly, the therapist who was assisting Lea with the Brunswick milieu). The children were taken from her and placed in a home in that milieu with the father and his new partner. Another boy whose troubled mother was similarly judged unfit, was taken by a couple and raised as their own.

One young woman who moved over to the milieu to live with and support the children recalled,

> "In the house where I lived, all of the people there were good with kids, so I learned a lot. It was solid and wholesome. But I saw bad things happening with other families. I made myself a promise that I would never have a child in a house group setting. Families are fragile in general unless you have a strong, loving, extended network. Living as we did right with the families, their problems were readily apparent. If people were too quick to point these out, the parents could only be made to feel guilty. Anyone may not be the best parent or be doing the best job, but the bottom line is that kids would rather have their own parents with them. Instead of supporting

people with their problems, there was a lot of criticism, a looking for perfection where it couldn't exist."

Another woman who moved into the Brunswick milieu in 1971 remembers that,

> "All of the action then was oriented to building the Willow, so we didn't have many groups. The milieu focused around the families and the children who lived there. I was involved with them. The families lived in a fish bowl in that setting and were greatly interfered with. Some parents had problems, but to my knowledge there was never any outright abuse. If it was judged that a mother, for example, was not sufficiently present to her child emotionally, that could be seen as sufficient cause to find another parent for him or her. It would be said that that woman should not have had children."

This happened to one family in the following manner: the relationship between the parents was coming apart and the mother was deeply shaken. Her therapist believed that she was not then able to provide emotionally for her children. She was convinced to leave the family and to stay at the farm for a time, accompanied by her therapist. Speaking of this family in the seminar, Lea decided spontaneously that one of the learning therapists would be very good with children. A report had been circulated that another one of the fathers had hit his son, so she designated the learner as the new therapist in charge of that child. Saying that he ought to work with more than one child, she assigned him the younger of the two boys whose mother had just been taken away. The boys were separated, the older one moving in with another family that had a daughter of similar age. The younger boy, a four year old, was moved over to the house group where his new "therapist" lived and was cared for by a succession of well-meaning volunteers. This was originally intended as a temporary measure, but it went on indefinitely. Later, the boy lived for several years with a couple who were willing to give him a home. The scars of his removal from his formerly intact family at such a young age remain with him to this day. A woman who was involved in the boy's life from that day (and who remains an important friend to him) remembers that the learner who was assigned this role,

> "was a decent person but he had no training or experience with children, yet he was suddenly the boy's therapist. People were brought in from all over the community to take care of the boy. I went over a couple of nights a week to put him to bed. He didn't know any of us. It was so destructive. His parents just vanished. His father was so angry with everyone that he disappeared from the boy's life at that point. Children were seen as disposable. It was all Lea's decision."

Looking back on this period, she is appalled by the things that happened. She realizes that she went along with Lea's decisions, doing her best to be helpful in any situation despite an inner sense of discomfort with what she saw around her.

> "I don't ever remember having doubts about Lea. If I did I certainly buried them. I had lots of doubts about myself. I always thought there was something wrong with me, that I couldn't fit in though I tried harder and harder. I bought the whole myth, but I felt terribly at odds with the world."

ML who worked closely with Lea, was called upon to implement or to defend decisions that Lea made, also says that if she had doubts about any decision,

> "I would feel that she was right, and I was wrong. I had no confidence at all. That was the tragedy of my therapy with her. She was not able to give me any confidence in myself, and I think that unconsciously she deliberately did that to keep people dependent on her. She brought me to a certain point but then wouldn't go any further. She wouldn't set a person free."

It was within the context of Lea's "work" and methods with families in the Brunswick milieu and elsewhere, that the Therafields school developed. So many parents and their therapists and helpers were in various ways held in thrall to Lea's imprimatur, to the by then infamous "Lea says!" that the gradual manoeuvring of her son Malcolm to seize control over the children was of a piece with directions long set in motion.

Lea and her Children

Lea with Rob and Josie

In the early days, Lea would speak of her two older children in quite glowing terms: Josie, the lovely and talented singer and Malcolm, the mathematical genius. Just as Lea presented her own family of origin in pristine terms, so she depicted her children and her relationships with them. The reality was much more troubled. At that time, Malcolm was studying at Queen's University. He was barely on speaking terms with her and Josie. He had not introduced Judy, his new wife, to his family. Josie, who had been openly rebellious with and contemptuous of her mother as a teen, had gone to England, trying to start a singing career. Lea was unsettled about them, feeling the guilt that any parent has over problems with her children. She was aware of the toll taken on them by the vicissitudes of the family's life in England and in Canada, and she longed to be able to repair the damage. She was undoubtedly pained by the realization that many in her practice were making strides to resolve residues of their own family backgrounds, becoming free to live productive and happier lives.

As I have written above, Lea's boundaries in dealing with people were, unfortunately, not very good. She would become involved in various ways in the personal lives of her clients, seeing these interventions for their good -- as they sometimes were. However, because she had developed such faith in her instincts, interventions could easily verge on outright interference. There are many difficult moments in the life of a parent with a child. One is the time when a parent must allow the child to forge his or her own way in the world precisely without the kind of interference that can bind the child to an adolescent state of dependency. Lea wanted too badly to make things better for her children and her interventions on their behalf had disastrous results for all involved. The adage "be careful what you wish for" was in this situation, spot on.

At Christmastime, 1965 Josie had come home for a visit. Then twenty years old, she had been living in England for over a year and had every intention of returning. Contracts had been signed for the spring; England was now her home. But Lea was worried about her. She was a very young woman living a long way away. She had been involved in relationships that would give most mothers pause. Lea was keen to keep her in Canada and to involve her with people in her new learning group. Every inducement was attempted. Josie was a recent convert to Catholicism and Greg Baum was to her a hero. If she joined the learning group, she would get to know him personally. People from 55 and 59 Admiral (prompted by Lea) introduced the topic of the learning group into conversations, saying how excellent it would be for her. As Lea's daughter, she received attentions from some of the men in the group. None of these inducements swayed her, however. What changed her mind was a scenario in which Lea used the influence of one of her clients to get Josie an audition. This led to a union job, and a contract for a gig on Avenue Rd. In the event, however, the job fell through and Josie was unable to claim her rights in the situation because the booking agent was her mother's client.

In the meantime, Josie had committed to remaining in Toronto. Lea had sent her to Tom for a battery of psychological tests, necessary she said for the kind of self-knowledge one ought to have when entering the learning group. Tom scheduled a series of meetings with her to "explain the results of the tests," though this was in fact her introduction to therapy. When he became attracted to her, Tom withdrew from that role, becoming before long her fiance and then, husband. Lea organized a "family group" for Rob, Josie, and herself as a locale for Josie's therapy. Others closer to the family like Tom were invited to participate to lend greater "objectivity" to the endeavour. When Malcolm and Judy landed in Toronto late in 1968, Judy was included in the group and Malcolm attended sometimes.

Clearly this was never a situation in which issues could be discussed openly and fully. So much of Lea's history and troubles were hidden from all present, even from herself. The others were either her children, her clients, or her students. Tom wasn't entirely in any of these categories, but he was her son-in-law and he carried to the end of his life a strong belief in her judgment. In these groups, Lea would baldly confront Josie about things she wasn't happy about. Attempting to do therapy with one's own mother, a mother with whom one had had an uneasy relationship, would be hard for anyone. Josie found it, "horribly, horribly painful. It was all difficult. It was flaming hot. My mother could be very hard on me in those settings though I don't think it was because of any ill will. I think it was just an impossible situation from any point of view." However, Josie joined the seminar and began to see clients, gradually developing a practice. When she and Tom moved into 105 Admiral in 1967, they were the house group therapists to the other, newer people who shared the first and second floors.

None of Lea's children could receive therapy of any depth within the Therafields fold. Given the circumstances, they would have had to go to people outside for objectivity and for a chance to explore their complex relationships with their parents, particularly with Lea herself. But this was never going to happen. There was "therapy" of a sort, looking at this but not that, going along so far but not beyond. Always in the foreground was the reality of their roles, their positions as part of "The Family." As her children took on more visible functions, Lea had more deliberately to enlist their public solidarity. Josie believed that it would be "unseemly, destructive even," for her to question or oppose her mother in any public forum. For all her promotion of confrontation as the new golden rule of therapy, Lea herself did not handle it well. She would not only defend her positions but would gather supporters to refute any challenges made. Others might be confronted, but by affiliation with Lea, Rob, Barrie, Josie, Malcolm, Visvaldis, or any other favourite of hers, could not. People learned that attempts of this kind led to having the tables turned against them. One would be variously accused of destructiveness, paranoia, or ignorance. As Lea had more and more issues in her own private life and those of her children to protect, open and free discussion within the seminar necessarily dried up.

Josie was in the anomalous position of being lauded in public and scolded in private. During the years of Therafields Josie said,

> "I could never question my mother, certainly in any public
> way. Permission wasn't there at all. I dreaded having
> daughters because I thought that my relationship with my
> mother wasn't so much bad as unexplored. I feared that
> whatever was there would be acted out in some dramatic
> manner with a girl that wouldn't happen with a male
> child."

In fact, Josie believed that her relationship with her family essentially ended once Therafields began.

> "It all had to do with the fish-bowl effect, the sense of
> always interacting in a public place, of there always being
> an audience. In my dealings with my family 90% of the
> time, if anything came up between my mother and me,
> it couldn't be dealt with naturally. Years earlier we might

have just gotten into a fight and then gotten over it. But within the Therafields context everything had weight and meaning. It's true that people couldn't confront me the way they might have someone else, but it was also true that if they had done so we couldn't have just had it out. I was in the position of trying to be a therapist in every situation."

This is a particularly sad commentary. It reflects how Lea viewed her own life as it evolved in that same fish-bowl. But the bowl grew naturally from the fact that Lea did not have a life of her own separate from her work, her clients and her students. Her homes were used by these same people to such an extent that real privacy was impossible. Josie also chose to live in large houses with other Therafields people even after the birth of her children. Like her mother, she enlisted impressionable, often vulnerable people to assist not just with the care of her children but also of herself and her home. Lea drew Josie into the work that she was doing, though not for the best of reasons. Lea was trying to make up for things that Josie had lacked in her earlier life. To her familiars, Lea would speak about her regret that she hadn't been able to provide the 'upper-class experience' that her children ought to have had. Within Therafields, she gradually tried to make that happen for them. Josie felt pressured by expectations that came her way because she was her mother's daughter. She had to live up to her position and then she began to capitalize on it. Over time Josie developed a "court" comparable to her mother's. And always in this court, like her mother, she remained the ultimate arbiter, always the "therapist," always unassailable.

Calling Josie "the therapist" though is a misnomer. It was simply that she took control of any situation that she found herself in, deferring only to her mother and her brother, Rob. She had learned enough of the discourse of therapy to be able to use it for her own purposes -- for flattery, to punish, or to soften the needs of daily life. She had never learned or appreciated therapy as a dispassionate relationship with another for the good of the other. At a marathon in the early 70s, Lea was preparing a new group of learners to begin seeing clients. A number of the already-working therapists were at the marathon. Lea invited any of them to say something to the new people about how they had prepared themselves to begin working. Josie immediately spoke up about how excited she had been when invited to start seeing people, saying that she had spent the whole previous weekend before her new clients came purchasing professional-looking clothes. There was a silence in the group after this comment. I don't remember if anyone else spoke about their preparation after this astonishing statement.

Josie's clients were eased into roles as baby-sitters, house-cleaners, drivers, masseuses, in one case, as a lover. She seemed to believe that merely being in her presence, within her ambience, would impart special value to the fortunate client-cum-servant. And like her mother, she would brook no opposition. Even the mildest complaint would be turned back on the complainant as an indication of serious faults of one's own. In the process the individual would be humiliated, shamed, and controlled. I don't think that Josie ever understood how she had used and abused people. Even as Therafields was falling apart in the early 1980s, and the dynamics became clearer to formerly foggy-minded people like myself, she remained puzzled by animosity that came her way. She would approach people asking to renew friendships though no relationship of that kind had ever existed. Around that time, Josie connected with musicians in Toronto and enjoyed working once again with her earlier passion, though she also continued to see new clients.

When Malcolm came back to Toronto with his wife, Judy, late in 1968, only a visit was planned. They were en route to Manitoba. He had completed a bachelor's degree at Queen's University, a master's in Windsor, and he was enrolled in the PhD program at Penn State. When they arrived here, however, Malcolm seemed to be experiencing a kind of break-down. Judy, meeting his family for the first time, was very taken with Lea and Robbie. She pressured Malcolm to remain and to receive therapy. Malcolm worked for a while with Tom; Judy saw Lea. Lea (or more likely, Therafields) purchased 61 Admiral, giving Malcolm and Judy the third-floor apartment and inducing some of the Hypno I people to move in with them. She dearly hoped that her son could be helped in ways that would solve some of his troubles and diminish his estrangement from the rest of the family.

Lea would speak in groups sometimes about the early life of the family during the war when they lived in Yorkshire. Because Harry could not find sufficient work, she had taken a job, leaving Malcolm as an infant with one or more local women. She worried about damage this might have done to him and speculated about the possibility that he had been sexually molested at some time in that period. She spoke also about the way that Harry would take up each child in turn as the centre of his life, only to abandon him or her when the next came along. Moreover, she said, Harry would make complaints about her to the children, turning them against her. Of the three children, Malcolm would possibly have been most subject to the difficulties experienced by and between Lea and Harry after the war and during the transition to their new life in Canada. He was a socially awkward child, brighter than most kids; his interests were different, and he was not a handsome boy. At school, he never really belonged, and he had a terrible time. Only at university did he begin to feel respected and understood. Within the family, he had taken the role of supporting his father, believing that Harry's life had been ruined by the move to Canada. This estranged him from the other two who, as their parents' marriage deteriorated, showed less respect for their father. Malcolm nursed resentment and outright contempt for Josie and Lea.

There was another component of the family experience that was spoken of at the famous Bigwin Island marathon over a year before he and Judy came to Toronto. Malcolm had evidently abused both Josie and Rob when they were younger. Whatever the details or substance of this report, they were known to all present and they were not introduced as a concern years later when Malcolm's take-over of the developing school for Therafields children became a fait accompli.

Soon after his arrival in Toronto, Malcolm became a presence on the tiny strip of Admiral Rd close to 61. He and Judy got jobs, though his lasted only a brief time. Malcolm had a great deal of trouble getting along with others in any work situation. His arrogance and contempt easily came to the surface making co-workers uneasy and angry. After this attempt at working, I don't know if Malcolm held other jobs before his involvement in the education of the children around 1973-4. His relationship with Judy was unravelling and he was attracted to the young women at 55, 59, and 32 Admiral, having affairs with a few. It can be said that at this point Malcolm was rather attractive, clever, somewhat charismatic like his mother when he so chose, and, charming and funny under the right conditions. Undoubtedly, the women drawn to him responded to these inducements though at the same time they were aware of his mother and his wife in the background. A woman who lived at 63 Admiral said to Malcolm that she found his running after these young women reprehensible, an insult to his wife with whom he was living. Others present at the time, men who belonged to the seminar, said nothing. The issue was clearly not to be spoken of.

Meg, also resident there, recalled that, "Once, I came back from the farm feeling insecure. I was quite uneasy around Malcolm. He came into my room and made overtures to me as though I was a little girl. He said that he would make me feel better by taking me for a walk in the woods and holding my hand. This didn't make me feel secure at all. He seemed drawn to women who were going through little girl feelings." Malcolm was sexually active at the time, pursuing a number of young women, but Lea didn't want to hear about it. This is an early example of the latitude given to Malcolm though allowed to no other. Any other married man trolling for the affections and passions of a series of immature women would have been confronted and curtailed. Tom, briefly his therapist, whose marriage to Josie had recently come apart, seemed amused by Malcolm's behaviour. "Maybe he's got it right," Tom said to me.

Malcolm attended the family group for a time, where Lea would confront him and Josie about equally. Malcolm considered some of the things happening in Therafields at that period to be misdirected. He was against the development of an entrenched community. He thought that the position Rob had been given by his mother was ruining him. He wanted Rob to leave home, to go away to university. He took Lea on over these issues and received abuse from her and others as a result. Though Lea would confront Malcolm in the family groups, she would support him in public. Other people could not successfully confront him as he simply would not take it. He would become angry and defensive and as Lea would not support the confrontation, it inevitably would fall flat. Over time if people spoke to Lea about him, she would ask why they were telling her their complaints. Did they not know that he was her son? Throughout, she was in a constant state of guilt and worry about him. As she seemed unable to influence him herself, she asked ML to be his periodic counsellor, a listener to his grievances. Malcolm never actually sought her out as a therapist, though he would phone her from time to time to vent some of his frustrations. Moreover, Malcolm was never part of a standard, house, or learning group where people could collectively address him about their concerns. Malcolm had more of his mother's temperament and potential – a bright flame that could lead him to his own vision. That kind of child likely needs more attention to help him along and keep him in the real world. He needed a different kind of father than Harry.

Lea related more closely to Rob than to either of her other children. But she poured so much into him. He became in some way her consolation, the more emotionally stable husband. He was parentified in that way. None of Lea's children had the kind of boundaries that they needed.

I first became aware of Rob when he came to our Tuesday-Friday group one evening in mid-1967 with his mother. He was then a tall, awkward, impossibly homely, teenage boy, given to outbursts of high-pitched laughter, who smiled a lot in a self-conscious manner. People in the group who had been with Lea for some time were clearly fond of him. This was the boy who but a few months later was given, with Barrie, charge of the administration of the already mushrooming entity of Therafields. Over the next eight years, Rob grew into his body and into his position, but never attained any substantial separation from his mother or from his family dynamics.

In the mid-1970s Rob would jokingly call himself the Prince of Mono Mills, a reference to the position in which he found himself at the right hand of his mother. The joke contained his awareness of privilege bestowed not because of merit, but simply, as in any royal family, from the right of primogeniture. Like Josie, Rob fully enjoyed his special position and its perks, but unlike his sister, could never quite escape from his knowledge of how they had come to him. In his turn, Rob became a therapist, but his work was an extension of his role in the family – the appeaser, the joker, the guy trying to make things seem OK. This is not a good description of a psychotherapist, who must at times stand firm, as might a good parent, in the face of tendencies or behaviours of a child. Rob acknowledged to me, when I spoke with him in 1997, that he always wanted a client to leave a session feeling better than when they entered it.

A woman who was working with Rob in the early days of her therapy said that she had come to Toronto at the behest of her brother, knowing that she needed help. Living in a house group on Admiral Road and caught up with the activities of the farm, she was able to push away her troubles, and just be a part of the community. Working with Rob, she said, that was easy to do – to simply pretend that she didn't have problems. He wanted her to feel good, so she did – at least on the surface of herself.

Rob was given a salary as he moved into the developing role as president of Therafields. He favoured sports cars, comics, and science fiction movies. He had the pick of the many beautiful and interesting women of the community, partnering over the years with several. His job was easy in the beginning. One woman, who struggled with a variety of short-term jobs in the couple of years that she was involved with Rob, was amazed at the little time that was required of him. He spent a lot of time in bed, she recalled, and was always available for whatever fun was happening.

As Therafields evolved and became more institutionalized, however, Rob's role became demanding. He was involved in the complex financial workings of the business and its many components. His moral compass was a reflection of that of his mother. In the early years, Lea would often encourage people in her groups to be straightforward and honest. "To thine own self be true," and "I could not love thee half so well, loved I not honour more," were oft-heard quotes. Later, accommodations with truth and honesty were not simply allowed, but were advocated if the results favoured Lea's or Therafields' interests. Workers are needed at the farm, or, a particular person would be helpful at a 'project' in Florida. Call in sick to your job. What's important is to honour the needs of the community, the family, not those of the broader society in which you have your being. A slippery slope that over the years gave greater latitude for manipulation to those charged with managing the resources of the community.

'Work Therapy'

Building 'Striders,' the farm workshop

Working at the farm

There was an incessant development of work projects from the late 1960s onward. The farm, the Willow, the Dupont St offices, the Striders building, the greenhouse, and the constant up-grading and renovating of existing structures, required a massive involvement of volunteer labour. To rationalize and render its demands more palatable, work was conceptualized as a meaningful avenue to greater self knowledge and health, in other words, a form of therapy. Instead of going for a session with your group or your therapist, you could spend a day or a weekend at the farm with them, doing valuable work together and having sessions in the evenings to explore emotions related to work. A few of the seminar members volunteered (or were volunteered) to lead groups on the weekend after the work at either the farm or at the Centre.

The early efforts at the farm were begun enthusiastically by Lea's clients, keen to establish a place of our own. As the needs of the construction and renovation machine grew apace, enthusiasm gradually began to lag. A system of moral press-ganging was begun which started right at the top. Lea used every opportunity to speak in groups or in "emergency" meetings called in the city about the importance of work as a central element of our community. Members were encouraged to speak about their desire to work or to confess their failings to adequately contribute. Each of her learning groups was exhorted to take up the challenge of tackling projects that were unfinished. Their clients were to be brought up to the farm or to the Centre to help. They were to be taught that they had entered a working community and that a certain amount of participation would be required as partial payment for their therapy.

Lea would appeal to the men to be manly, to muscle up to the work, in a sense to prove their love for her, their faith in her, by being helpful in whatever desperate need was then being trumpeted. "Didn't they know that Visvaldis' attraction to the community had been because it was a working group?" This assertion inverted the actual progression of events as Visvaldis and Lea met and were drawn to one another before the purchase of the original work project: the farm itself. Moreover, though many of the improvements enhanced living and working conditions in the environment, they essentially stemmed from Lea's need to give Visvaldis a focus and a sense of purpose. Ultimately, the demands of the work projects drained the community not only financially but also morally and spiritually. The central vision of the early movement -to receive, learn about, and utilize psychotherapy in one's own life and, for some people, in helping others,- became mired in the constantly renewed demand for and conversation about physical work, by then an important end in itself.

An example of the kind of focus brought to bear about the need for volunteer work can be seen in a meeting held in the large group room of the Centre on Dupont St. in December, 1973. All working therapists were asked to show up that evening for a talk with Lea and Visvaldis about the current state of the work sites. Lea began by saying that the working side of the Therafields enterprise was in a sorry state. She went on to say, "All of us have the same feelings about the importance of physical work but we're not getting across to our dramists, (the word Lea had coined for clients), the importance of this aspect. When we got the farm, we at that moment committed ourselves to becoming a working group. There's no question about that, but when ten people show up to work instead of a hundred, it's ridiculous."

Rob spoke up to say that there were always lots of reasons why people slacked off work but that periodically we just need to have our butts kicked. He was clearly including himself in needing that treatment. Visvaldis then spoke about his view that,

"It seems that the pioneering spirit has gone after building the Willow. There seems to be no urge now for building offices for our therapists and the greenhouse up north is dragging. The work on Lea's office is slow. The spirit that was with us when the Willow was built is just not around. Not in too many. We should ask ourselves why this is so because it was really a dramatic experience there."

A few people spoke enthusiastically about the work projects and about getting their clients more involved, but as usual with these meetings, no real answer was given to Visvaldis' question: why had the spirit gone out of the work? Most present generally kept a low profile. No one came right out and said – "because we are tired of always having to work. We have other things in our lives that are important to us. We are constantly under pressure to perform and moreover, to pressure our clients into performing. We've had enough. Give it a break. Stop pushing more and more projects". To utter such truths would run counter to the myths that Lea and Visvaldis wanted to perpetuate.

Lea's initial statement underlines her determination and delusion, if in fact she really believed it, that "all of us," i.e., all there present, had the same feelings about the primacy of on-going physical work within our community. This particular meeting ended with Lea joking a bit and then saying, "I have a feeling that people are raring to go. Is this right or not?" From a few: "Oh, yes." Lea: "Would anyone here who is really interested in tackling this, utter some sound?" Great deal of sound then and laughter. Fade to black. Little accomplished.

A seminar member reflected later that

"The notion of work as a form of therapy had its good aspects. People said, 'We can make use of the work experience as a revelation of inner conflicts and work with them.' But soon there was pressure to exploit people who were in therapy to help with the building of facilities. There was quite a variety of ways that the therapists handled that pressure. I protected my groups. I gave speeches about people being able to come and work if they felt it would be good for them. I didn't want to use the super-ego. But that wasn't common. The stated position was to use the authority of the therapist and to get one's clients to go. So that was a bad scene."

The centrality of physical work had the effect of eroding the values and the spirit of the original group as well as diverting its energies and focus from its primary goals. Still many of the people whom I interviewed, particularly some of the men, spoke of the work scene as one of the things that they had most gained from during their time in Therafields. Working in construction and on the land with other men gave many their first experiences of manual, practical, labour. It nurtured in them a sense of competency and of manliness that carried over into their on-going lives. My brother, Craig, told me that,

"I found working at the Centre and the farm especially helpful. I had to really make myself do it at first. I hated it. But gradually I felt better and began to enjoy being there with the other men, making things and learning things. Doing things with Dad had been terrible. I used to dread doing things around the house with him."

The Summer of Discontent: 1975

The summer of 1975 revealed a growing disunity within the heart of the Therafields', a breaking-down of what had been in the early-1970s, a more united community, on the whole satisfied with (or at least unquestioning of) the decisions being taken by Lea and her executive branch, and with the therapeutic directions being taken. But by that summer there were developing clues that Lea was succumbing to her own mental health problems. Though this was not explicitly formulated, nor openly discussed, a few, like her son Rob, were aware of problems.

AXIS, a 'workbook' publication for members of the learning groups had been initiated in December 1969. The December 1974 edition contained a piece written by Lea, entitled, "A Silhouette." In it some details of Lea's marriage to Harry, who had died not long before, were revealed. It was enthusiastically received in the community. The article was well-written and, importantly, it gave many people not close to Lea or her family, a more personal sense of her and her life. Encouraged by the response, Lea continued to write, publishing in the February 1975 AXIS, "A Year in the Life of a Young Girl." Rob was already aware of and concerned about disturbances in his mother that were affecting her behaviour and judgment. There was never a question of her seeing a therapist outside the community, let alone a psychiatrist for a diagnosis of her trouble. Rob believed that she needed to get away from the pressures of the community and "encouraged," even pushed her into going to Florida to focus on writing. This seemed to be a satisfying and even therapeutic endeavour for her.

During the two week long 1975 CAG/seminar marathon, which Lea did not attend, there was a great deal of talk about finances and responsibilities. Over the late 1960s and the early 1970s, the constant stream of people looking for therapy had kept the money situation fairly buoyant. But in 1975 this flow began to ebb, putting pressure on the administration to generate further funds to cover the overhead of what had become an expensive operation, or, to cut costs. It had always been difficult for the seminar to find out what money came in and how it was spent. Rob and Barry, with the addition of Rik, the company accountant, made decisions, allocated resources, and kept details to themselves and Lea. But by this point the therapists who were working long hours to generate the income were not happy with its distribution nor with the lack of information about how financial decisions were made. They wanted answers. A core of the original Hypnotherapy group had by then matured considerably in their skills and practices. Still, confronting Lea directly about money issues would not have been easy for them given their histories with her. They were not, however, so hesitant to chase after Rob about them. Their more open demands were likely facilitated by the fact that Lea was not present that summer.

Like the watershed moments of 1967-8 -- the Bigwin marathon, the acquisition of the farm, and the new administration of what had been Lea's private practice, this break in Lea's -until then- investment in the on-going business and development of the Therafields organism, can in hindsight be seen as another substantial break. For the next couple of years, Lea travelled back and forth from Florida to Toronto and the Willow, writing a series of books, dropping in on marathon groups, and encouraging some of the projects that Visvaldis was espousing. The books were patently autobiographical, though somewhat removed from actual details. They were sometimes rewritten in fantasy as in the volume entitled "The Way It Might Have Been," the altered story of a love affair that had ended badly before Lea married Harry. The publication of her books and how people received them in the community became for Lea a major focus, testing relationships with persons who had been her clients and colleagues for well over a decade. This endeavour was frankly embarrassing for many. Some people were praising the books as a revolutionary form of literature, a new genre that used stories to reveal complex psychological aspects of the lives of characters. Lea basked and preened in the aura of their acclaim. A system of purchase was devised whereby individuals could acquire the volumes as they were produced, paying so much per month over time.

In truth, the books did not deserve the high praise given. They were adequate stories, somewhat sentimentalized, and reasonably well-written, but by no means major works of art. All of Lea's writings were thinly disguised apologia for her own life and work. It is hard to find anything remotely like a confessional note in her work. Susan, her protagonist and alter-ego, is portrayed as the universally good woman, one who struggles valiantly against all odds, all evils, and prevails through her own intelligence, courage, and creativity. This is not said to denigrate the reality of these aspects of Lea herself. She was intelligent, courageous, and creative. But that was only a part of her truth. She had her own dark and secret places that she was unwilling or unable to share in any effective manner to receive help. It's not that these elements went unexpressed. But, they were revealed only to people who were in some manner dependent upon her and in no position to challenge her increasingly disturbed behaviour. This was particularly true in the late 1970s as Lea moved closer toward the total collapse that engulfed her in the early 1980s. People who read her books and could not judge their worth along the lines being promoted, found themselves unable to speak about their reactions openly. But Lea, sensitive as always to nuance, knew who liked her work and who didn't. This division added another level to an already developing fear that she had of people being against her in a quite personal manner.

Without Lea's energetic presence, the fissure growing between the interests of the administration and those of the therapists, became more overtly evident. The small group that began lobbying Rob to open the books, were aware that Lea had been granted a salary of $90,000, an unheard-of amount in comparison with the salaries of even the most senior and hardest working therapists. From this she paid a stipend to those who worked for and travelled with her. Much of their sustenance – room and board, for example, was absorbed by the usual running costs of the Willow. Visvaldis was also receiving a generous salary. What else was happening to the large pocket of money that was submitted by clients every month? They wanted to know.

In 1970, the Therafields Corporation had been created to facilitate some of the movement of money and properties. Various pockets were used in ways to benefit Lea and her immediate family without any accounting to the members who were in fact footing the bill. Visvaldis had been promoted by Lea as a visionary architect. However, his good ideas could be undermined by the fact that he needed supervision himself in keeping projects on course, limiting them to a manageable scale given the financial and human resources available. I have written above of the solution found when the cost of the Willow renovations outstripped Lea's sources. Therafields coffers were opened to pay for them. That detail was not mentioned explicitly when the prospect of a joint venture was discussed in the seminar and in groups. This was a further mixing of Lea's private estate with that of Therafields.

A few years later the Willow was sold by Lea to Therafields, a tidy deal which allowed her to buy two adjoining condos at the Palace Pier. A clause of the sale agreement gave Lea the right to live at the Willow for the remainder of her life notwithstanding the sale. The Palace Pier apartments were combined to make one enormous unit, renovated like the Willow at the expense of Therafields and by the volunteer labour of its members. Again, the idea was floated that the gigantic apartment could be used as a site for future meetings of the seminar and other groups. When Lea died in 1987, Rob inherited the place, benefiting not only from equity gained by his mother's earlier labours, but by the financial and physical output of Therafields members.

In late 1973, Therafields Foundation, a non-profit organization, had obtained charitable status from the federal government. Its charter's aims were listed as: the promotion of research in the areas of emotional development, life styles, environment, and creativity. Principal officers had to be named on the papers going to Ottawa. They could not be the same as those of the administrative officers (Rob, Barrie, and Rik) of the incorporated Therafields. Those named were: Visvaldis, president; John D, manager. Dan McDonald and Larry Rooney were asked to also lend their names to the Foundation's patent. Dan recounted though that,

> "We were told right from the beginning by Lea and
> Visvaldis that these were purely legal titles. They would

carry no authority. It was couched nicely: 'The way we do things, the way we run things.' Larry and I both knew that there was little we could do about it. But when Visvaldis died in 1983, we had to go in and clean the whole thing up. He had used it as his own personal bank account. He was the president and Larry and I were the vice-president and treasurer, but we were never consulted on anything. We knew nothing about what was happening. Earlier the farm had been deeded to the Foundation. Rob made the decision, but no one was ever asked about it. The Hypno I people had bought the farm, but the records had been lost showing who had put in money."

A man who had spent much of his professional career working with and studying not-for-profit groups reflected that

"in Therafields there was never even a minimal level of democratic practice. In other groups, like the United Church ministry for example, people add up the money now and then and give a financial accounting. I went to Rik once and argued for some accountability to the people who were paying fees, paying the rent, and contributing their time to work. I said that we should be told where the money was going and that there ought to be some collective decision-making mechanism about how it was spent. He made it clear that I was wrong, that it wasn't any of my business. Later I realized that I had always been given that message, 'Hey, mind your own business; don't interfere.' Not being in the seminar made it seem even less my business, but most people in the seminar didn't know what was happening either."

When Rob was approached by some of the therapists about the finances, he would appear to be compliant, making promises of a reveal that never actually came to pass. This struggle led to difficult scenes with Rob and sometimes with Lea over the next several years. One of the therapists remembered that

> "when I complained to Lea that Visvaldis was receiving a salary double that of the hardest-working therapist though he did no work, she said that it was my problem with my father. Regardless of what problems I might have had with my father, we were taken for a ride with Visvaldis. We were asked to pay him a large salary on the basis that for a couple of years he had donated his services. After this he did little. Lea and Rob covered for him and no one did anything about it. Any effort would bring forth pretty dire threats from Lea."

It's revealing that this man spoke with Lea about his unhappiness with Visvaldis' salary but did not, possibly could not, dispute her own.

To the end of Therafields as a discrete entity, the "administration," specifically Rob and Rik, stonewalled attempts for an accounting of its affairs. But because of the pinch in meeting operating costs, finances became a central theme of the 1975 summer marathon. Not wanting to give an open accounting, the administration began to search about for places to lay blame. 'Why was the running of the farm and other properties in the country so expensive? Were Therafields' staff giving value for their pay rates?' Each employee was put on notice that at a certain date, their jobs would be terminated. Each would then be interviewed to determine if he or she ought to be re-hired, based on a full explanation of their roles and responsibilities.

Clearly, this was playing dodge-ball. At the farm, for example, employees were paid very low salaries, 80% of which was gathered back to pay for their rooms and board. Working long hours with barely a day off, these people could truly be called wage-slaves. Each wanted to be there, chose to be there, because of their own interests and inclinations, and, in great part because of their commitment to Lea and to Therafields as the community and family they had always wanted. When they did decide to move on from this work, or when as in the 1980s, the community came apart and the rural properties were sold, most walked away literally with nothing: no savings, no equity, no pensions, not even with much personal furniture. Because Rob, Lea, and Rik resisted an opening of the books, in the summer of 1975 the rural staff was subjected to a torturous exercise of justifying their employment.

It was a classic case of the big chiefs getting the cream, and the "little guys" getting the dregs. Rob, Lea, and Visvaldis were given salaries far exceeding those of the therapists, and many multiples more than the workers at the farm and in the city who took care of their every need. Once expenses were tabulated for feeding and caring for the farm and for the Willow, discrepancies became clear. At the farm, for example, food prepared and served to the week-day staff and to the volunteers who came on the weekends, was vegetarian. It consisted mainly of vegetable soups, salads, and multi-grain bread. At the Willow, considerably more lavish meals were served. As well, fruit bowls, chocolates, even cigarettes for Visvaldis were provided on the Therafields' ticket. The difference between the cost/person of those staying at the Willow and those at the farm was enormous.

That year some of Lea's early clients, people who had been supportive of her and her projects and upon whom she counted, began to pull away from the core. John N and his wife, Jerry Laughlin, June and Vlad H, Tom McNeil, and others, moved out their house groups to private residences, generally reducing their involvements with Therafields. Threatened by their loss, Lea began to speak of this group and others who were pulling away, as 'paranoid.' Jokes were initiated by Rob and Barrie, who did not take Lea's identification of the group too seriously, about the Panorama apartment complex into which some had moved, calling it 'Paranoid Towers.'

For a few years, John N had been connected with the Findhorn community in Britain and had attempted to bring into Therafields some of its vision and spirit. This had utterly failed, however, as Lea and Visvaldis had shown no interest in or appreciation of the group. John was frustrated with the on-going demand for more and more building projects emanating from Visvaldis, particularly his oft enunciated call for a large 'environmental centre ' in the country. It was clear to John that the spirit earlier felt within the Therafields community was waning and that there was no longer any clear vision animating it. He had initially placed himself more or less at the disposal of Lea to further the aims of the community – building or renovating properties in the city and the country, and taking on responsibilities for clients and groups. When John pulled back, giving himself space to find new directions, Lea, who had depended on him for practical and emotional support for over a decade, was stricken by what seemed to her an apostasy.

The Therafields' School

In 1975, another component of the Therafields' landscape pushed its way into general consciousness as a school, begun in 1973 for some of the children of Therafields members, began a part-time residency at the farm. Jim Healy's younger sister, Sharon, had come to Toronto in the late 1960s to do some therapy in the then developing Therafields. During her stay, she lived in a house group, saw a therapist, and at the same time was trained in the Montessori method of teaching. When her training was completed, she took a job in Kitchener for a year. In 1973, some of the parents in the large Brunswick milieu approached Sharon, asking her to start a school with their kids. They wanted a system that closely reflected their philosophy of living, one that would be more sensitive to the individual needs of the children than was the public system as they were then experiencing it. Sharon was delighted and keen to work with them. They began with nine kids, using the basement of 477 Brunswick Ave., and having full use of the enormous open space behind the houses on Brunswick and Kendal as well. Over the next year or two Sharon's school continued in this fashion.

In the meantime, Malcolm had become interested in education as his infant daughter grew older. He read widely about schooling and had interesting and innovative ideas about ways that it could be conducted. His own early education had been an unhappy experience; no doubt he wished to avoid that fate for his daughter. Josie and Lea were keen to have him work with the young children as they came along and some of the Brunswick parents were interested in his ideas as well. He began to do 'classes' with the older kids at Sharon's school. In September 1974, ML moved back to Toronto from the farm and Malcolm began a more structured involvement with her two children, Josie's son, and his daughter.

Soon afterwards, pressure began to build, especially from Lea and Josie, to amalgamate the two small schools into one with both Malcolm and Sharon as teachers. Lea was happy to see Malcolm involved in a project that she believed in and that he seemed well suited for. It gave him a focus, a job, and a legitimate role within Therafields. Josie, who was Sharon's therapist at that time, brought pressure to bear on her to go along with the idea of one school. Sharon thought then that it was probably a positive step for the kids. She liked Malcolm and his ideas. At the same time, she was nervous about him.

The amalgamation was affected by early 1975. It was decided to bring the newly-formed school, then generally called the Therafields school, to the farm. The kids were bused up from the city on Tuesday mornings with a few of the parents attending. They slept over a couple of nights with the older kids at the renovated former schoolhouse just down the road from the farm, though later, in the dorms of the barn with the younger ones. They had classes in the group room and outdoors and would return to the city on Thursday afternoons. Some of the younger children had difficulty making the transition to sleeping in the dorms, but the older kids loved it all. It was a great adventure. They would meet in the group room, sitting in a circle while Malcolm talked with them. They had spelling bees and would act out scenarios on the stage in the upper barn. There was a structure to the day and within it they were learning and having a lot of fun.

One of the older girls remembers:

> "It was so beautiful up there. In general, the kids were smart and interested in a lot of things. We would be outside all day, wandering in the fields and the woodlot. We older kids would sleep at the schoolhouse. After dinner, we would all walk down there through the woods, the sun going down behind us. It was so beautiful. Sharon was a part of the school then and she was terrific. Malcolm was great too at that phase. Everyone was into it in a special way and it was fun getting to know the people at the farm. One of the great things about being there was the focus on nature, the garden, the greenhouse. We were lucky to

be there with other kids of all ages. We never wanted to go back to the city."

Other experiences at the farm were not as wholesome, however. There were attempts to do some group therapy with the kids. Each week they would be gathered in the group room for a session -- sometimes all the kids, but more often just the older ones. The girl quoted above told me,

"There seemed to be an assessment that some of the kids were problem children. I think it was quite arbitrary, bearing no relation to their actual emotional make-up. I was always skeptical and irritated by all the therapy stuff. I thought it was a lot of shit and that a lot of it was just made up. In the groups, I would steel myself to being attacked or to watching someone else being attacked. The group leaders (two or more members of the seminar) would direct the conversation. They would decide to talk to one kid and would bring up something that had happened and get some other kid to say something to him or her about it. Before long whoever was being focused on would be crying. Once you reached the point of crying or raging, they would say: there, there. That's what they wanted. I never did it though. I would think -- what is it about these people?"

Malcolm was not in favour of these meetings though they bear a resemblance to his own practices with the children in later years.

Not all the parents in the Brunswick milieu had been happy about Malcolm joining the school begun by Sharon and by them. One recalled:

"When Malcolm first got involved, we had a so-called interview with him. I asked him what his qualifications were and he became livid. He mentioned OISE (the Ontario Institute for Studies in Education) and said that he'd done something there. In my opinion he had no educational expertise and little to offer. I should have sent up 18 red flags in the meeting and said, 'This is dumb. You don't trust your children to someone like him.' But I trusted Sharon and she really tried to make his involvement work. It just became a take-over though."

At the farm, tensions among different factions became palpable. There was a series of fraught exchanges in the dining room among the parents focusing mainly on the children's diet. At the time, Lea was talking generally about the importance of good food combining. Some parents became rigid about how this ought to be applied. No peanut butter with bread, but, peanut butter on celery sticks was allowable. All fruits and vegetables should be washed and peeled, or, washed in a particular manner and not peeled. As I was living at the farm that summer, I was privy to some of these conversations. Whatever the topic, one could sense a deeper, unspoken agenda that related more to the discomfort of some about their loss of autonomy with their children and the desires of others to go along with the directives of Malcolm and Lea.

At the same time, another situation central to the future of the school was being played out. Malcolm had flirted with, and had had liaisons with, at least a couple of the mothers. But he was becoming attracted to Sharon and wanted to develop a relationship with her. Lea was very keen for this to happen. She no doubt thought that Sharon would be good for Malcolm, a stabilizing factor in his life. She talked with her a couple of times, encouraging her to give him a chance. But Sharon wasn't interested. Malcolm accepted the rejection in seeming good part, but before long differences between them became more underscored. Sharon said later,

"Malcolm's revenge was simply to get rid of me and everyone else just hopped on the bandwagon. He had basically taken over the school once we were at the farm. Malcolm isn't a team player; he's basically into slave labour: you do this; I do nothing; but, I get all the credit. I forget what the ultimate issues were, but it came to a point where he and I parted ways over questions about the way the school should be run, who was going to put in the time, what the kids should be learning, and so on. Almost every issue became a controversy. But the real thrust from him was: this is my school. If you aren't going to be involved with me, then get out. Then all these supposedly impartial people like Lea and Josie got involved."

At a small meeting called at the farm, a decision to support Malcolm was made. Sharon was not invited to the meeting and was not consulted. She was simply informed that the school was now solely in Malcolm's hands. Josie, at the time Sharon's therapist, had not supported her.

"I felt very let down, especially by some of the Hypno I women who were involved in the school. I felt that they were just like sheep then, doing what they were told and afraid to go up against Lea. They basically railroaded me out of the school and out of the Brunswick learning group. Lea and Josie both told me that if I didn't want to go along with Malcolm that I was out of the group. They said that I was showing obvious signs of disturbance. It was all cloaked in terms of the school and how I didn't want to go along with the way he wanted to develop it. I realized then that Therafields had crossed a line and that Therafields and I were parting ways."

When Sharon left the school none of the kids was told that she had been ousted. Without explanation, she was just no longer there. One of the girls who had been with Sharon's school since she was six said,

"I had liked Malcolm at the beginning, but when Sharon left I felt some resentment towards him as I believed that she had left because of him. I remember thinking that there was something weird about the transition. We felt abandoned. She had been so good and so involved with us. We always had neat things to do in the Brunswick backyards. I was very sad when Sharon left as things were different without her. After she was gone we didn't have structured teaching. It was all very vague."

Another recalled: "When you are young as I was, nothing seems that unusual because you don't have a reference point. Sharon's gone -- OK. Still, it seems that a lot of the structure of the school changed or collapsed after Sharon left." Malcolm now had a quite free hand with the directions that the school would take.

Having Children

In the late 1960s and early 1970s, few children were born into the Therafields community. The focus of the community, especially within the various learning groups that Lea had formed, was turned toward working with clients and building the physical structures where therapy could be conducted. By that time, Lea had become intensely interested, obsessed even, about questions of successful motherhood. She would speak about it in groups. Once Lea's children had returned, not to live independent lives, but rather to her bosom, to the centre of the community in which she had developed her practice, her attention had turned strongly toward them. Her practice, her business, became the family business, ultimately providing jobs and status for all those closest to her -- Rob, Josie, Malcolm, and Visvaldis. Because she was unable to face honestly within herself or with others the true bases of her relationships with each of these people, dishonesty and manipulations by necessity multiplied. Her students and clients, still caught in the confusions of both positive and negative transference --longing for her love and approval, and, fearing her wrath and rejection-- stumbled along with her, supporting directions that she took.

Lea had spoken in glowing terms about her children, by extension about her own mothering, for years before Josie and Malcolm returned as adults involving themselves in the community that had become central to her life. The disparities between the myth and the realities became obvious to some of the people closest to her. Clearly Rob had not been traumatized in the ways that Malcolm and Josie had. They seemed to carry pieces of the family troubles that she had to protect so that those with whom she lived and worked would not know things about them and her. But the fact that Malcolm had abused Josie as a child, had been spoken of on the

Bigwin marathon. The two of them had left the family for some time but then came back. They were the ones that Lea became obsessed about saving herself from. It was them that she feared. If a woman had maternal failures and some bad things happened, some harming things, it would be very disturbing to her. Then if she starts something, and becomes the big resource and is looked at as an expert on families, she is vulnerable when the ghosts of her past begin to come home. When Josie was pregnant with her first child, Lea convened a Christmas project for her at the farm. A woman close to the family at the time said,

> "I think that Josie having a baby was scary for Lea. What kind of a mother would she be? All of her own experiences as a mother came crowding in on her."

Lea was living a double life. Inwardly, she feared facing or being faced with the troubles between herself and her children. Outwardly, she had assumed the mantle of the Great Mother, the ultimate source of knowledge and wisdom with respect to children and families. Over the 1970s her troubles grew into an obsession, not just with already formed families, but also with the question of whether or not various women ought to have children, or, having them, whether they ought to keep them. At a CAG marathon in November 1973, Lea asked the question: "How many people in this room feel that they should not have children?" She asked for a show of hands. She would then nod to a particular person and say, "Absolutely right. Right." To another, "I'm not sure about you. You're a bit young yet." To another, "I don't feel so badly about you." Some women not present were mentioned by her as clearly not being suitable though she said they made excellent helpers. She went on to say, "There are many women who would make very good mothers if they adopt a child. There are many women, who if they have a child, it's like they give something up. It's almost like they become husks. It's very sad."

Deciding whether or not to have a family became more than a personal issue for a couple. It became an act of daring, especially for women, a high wire act with enormous potential for failure. Over the next few years the sense emerged that few women were capable of being good mothers. A CAG woman recalls that,

"There was a craziness in Lea and in Josie about anyone having babies except themselves. All this was huge and horrible for CAG women. By that time only one had had a baby and she had been vilified and not helped at all. We were in our thirties then. We were caught in an odd obedience position because of all the questioning of whether we thought we could be good mothers. It was mad. You cannot mess with a woman's odyssey about whether to have children. It can take years. Even if someone concludes that she doesn't want to, there can be real grief and mourning about it."

Some women were actively discouraged from having children, being told that they were too paranoid. Others were told that their body-type indicated a poor outcome from a pregnancy. When one of Josie's 'friends' miscarried, Josie pronounced vehemently that anyone looking at that woman's body could see that she ought not have children. No concern or empathy for the heart-broken woman was in evidence. There gradually developed a feeling that only Lea's daughter, her daughter-in-law, and another woman close to the family could do well having children, and only then under Lea's close supervision. One member of CAG later commented, "It was like a bee hive. One female is fed the royal jelly and all the others are workers."

In 1975-6 a few children were born despite this confounding atmosphere. I was one of the new mothers. Lea resurrected a 1920s or 1930s British Mothercraft booklet and more or less demanded that its proscriptions be followed. Bran was to be cooked in the oven and sewn into a pillow case for the ideal infant mattress. Diapers must be of cloth; no plastic diaper covers were to be used, only knitted ones. There were to be nighties of a certain type, so many sweaters, blankets, and so on. Babies were to be placed in rooms with a particular kind of ventilation. Breast feeding was de rigeur, but only on a rigid four-hour cycle. Any woman having a baby during this period would hasten to subscribe to all and any measures suggested. An "inspection" of some nature could occur at any time. One woman's therapist (undoubtedly prompted by Lea) asked to come to see the arrangements for her coming child. While there the therapist pointed out to the expectant mother that there was a thin layer of dust on her furniture, not at all a good sign. The woman was careful to inspect her furniture closely after that reprimand, but she resented the inference.

After 1975, Lea was away a great deal but her obsession and interference with mothers and their babies had by no means abated. In 1978 another woman was struggling to bond with her child in its early months. Though in Florida at the time, Lea heard something of the woman's troubles and decided that she ought to give up her baby to another woman who 'really wanted a child.' When a visitor arrived at the Florida beach house, Lea grilled her about how the mother was doing. The visitor assured Lea that she was doing fine, but Lea was not interested in hearing that. She continued to speculate about who would be the best person to take the child. Lea telephoned me from Florida asking if I would be interested in taking on this baby. I knew nothing about the situation but I knew right away that I didn't want to do it. I thought that it was weird. I simply said that I'd have to talk it over with my husband. Lea didn't ask again though. There were at least two other women lobbying her for the child. Luckily for the mother, her therapist invited her to come to live at her house with the baby. She got other women to come and help, and before long, things righted themselves between mother and child.

The disturbance in Lea about mothers and babies came to a head when Rob's girl friend, Sheron became pregnant in 1978. Lea had tried to prevent their relationship, though when Rob persisted in it, she was at least on the surface accepting. When Sheron told Lea about the pregnancy, "The first thing she said to me was to ask if I had considered an abortion. I couldn't believe it! Then there was a rush to get us married right away. She was so concerned about how things were seen, and she feared a scandal."

Another woman in the seminar had become pregnant shortly before this. As the time came closer for the deliveries of these babies, Lea became more and more agitated. One of the women close to the family at that time said,

> "Lea had a fantasy of having another baby herself -- sort of
> like the old Abraham and Sarah thing. She was going a bit
> dotty then. She got on a huge bandwagon about Caron's

baby (not the woman's real name) because I think it was tied in some way to her fantasy of having the baby herself. She stormed over to Caron's house one day demanding to see her clothes for the baby. Caron was upstairs with all her helpers. They were doing this and that and Lea would say, 'Bring down the nightgowns! Bring down the sweaters!' It was really crazy."

Caron was already insecure enough about what she was doing. She had been elevated by Lea early-on to a special person status, becoming a therapist though she hadn't had much therapy herself. When the baby was born, a caesarean section was necessary. That shattered Caron. It wasn't part of the plan for the perfect baby and the perfect childbirth. Lea seized on the caesarean too as a way of discrediting her, saying things in the seminar like, 'She didn't want to give birth to the child.'

The shaming of Caron is an example of a pattern that Lea increasingly was using in her relations with people whom she had set up for initial success but whom she later undermined. In Caron's case it was accomplished publicly and brutally. Not only was Caron deemed not a good candidate for motherhood, her roles as a therapist and group leader were challenged. Dissatisfaction aired by her clients were broadcast. She was spoken of as a woman who had 'used' her clients in ways detrimental to their therapy. There may have been truth to these allegations, but it's rich to consider them from the perspective of the way in which Lea and Josie had themselves more overtly used clients.

Barrie had worked closely with Caron in a group that they took together. This must have been a particularly difficult moment for him: Lea was 'exposing' the culpability of a woman whom Barrie knew well and cared for. But his loyalty to Caron was exceeded by that to Lea. He went along with Lea's view, expressing his shock and dismay when learning of Caron's indiscretions. Caron and her husband moved out of their home and left behind what had been for both of them, a central place in the orbs of Lea and Therafields.

When Sheron's baby was born soon afterwards, Lea turned on her as well. Sheron recalled:

"I took it for about four weeks because I didn't know any better. When the baby was born, Lea called and said, 'I'm sending Stella over to stay with you for six weeks because you have no instincts.' She said she was very concerned about the baby because I was his mother. But there is never a time that you are more intuitive than when you give birth to a baby. She was into this whole thing about only feeding the kid every four hours. I had to sneak around to feed him when he needed it. She found me doing that one day and said, 'What are you, a cow?' After a few weeks, I said to Rob that it was all crazy. The child was crying, and Stella was walking him up and down and he needed to be fed. If you didn't follow the British Mothercraft manual, then you couldn't be the perfect mother. It was horrible for me. I hated her at that time and didn't want her in the house. I felt like she was insanely jealous of me, that I had stolen Rob from her. She couldn't join in and be a part of what was happening. She had to control it. That was the worst part of knowing her."

Late in 1977 Lea decided to start a parents' group for those in the seminar who by then had children. As my daughter, Elizabeth, had been born a year earlier, I was a member. Another parents' group, for the Brunswick-Kendal milieu, had been running for a few years. Lea may have attended the first meeting of the seminar group but if so, thereafter it was held at 105 Admiral in Josie's living room. It was presumed to be a meeting of colleagues and to not have a leader, but the truth is that from the beginning Josie tended to set the agenda. The group ran to sometime in 1980. (It may have continued in some form after that date, but when my second child was born that summer, I no longer attended.)

My husband, Maurice, rarely came because of his teaching schedule.

Attendance was expected and generally I did go, but in retrospect, I experienced it as oppressive. If there had been enough trust, caring, and good will among us to allow a real sharing of our experiences and trials as parents, it might have been of value. In the main I recall two themes: one was Josie calling someone to account: it could be Tom (father of her elder son), Adam (father of her younger son), or Judy (her sister-in-law). Others, including myself, received this treatment as well. The second theme related to the school, by the late 1970s called Ká school. Most of the parents in the seminar group had their children in the school, by then completely run by Malcolm.

Ka School

As the years passed, concerns about Malcolm raised in the parents' groups became more and more negative. Malcolm wanted parental involvement only to provide the most menial of services. Though the parents were highly-educated people, he refused to let them be teachers of the children. The kids were to teach each other. He didn't want any influences on them other than his own. After Sharon Healy left the school, it continued in part-time residence at the Therafields farm until Christmas time, 1976. In January 1977, the school was relocated to Toronto full-time with 59 Admiral Rd as the official and main location. At first the school was restricted to the large basement room, but later it was given rooms on the first floor as well. Malcolm had an office there. In the "greenhouse" room at the back of the house, the kids sometimes watched black and white movies. Malcolm's personal quarters were in the coach house at the rear.

As his antipathy toward Therafields had grown with time, Malcolm wanted to clearly distinguish the school as his own, not as it had earlier been called, the Therafields' school. He gave the school the name of Ka around that time. The word, taken from an ancient Egyptian religion, represents 'a life-force component of soul.' Malcolm's feelings about Therafields were by no means kept from the children in his charge. One of the older girls recalls: "Malcolm was very anti-Therafields. He hated it; he thought that the whole thing was evil and that everyone involved was a lemming."

Lea continued to worry about Malcolm. She had advocated his becoming a part of the school and then supported his take-over, but she felt that he was languishing. She believed that he had talent with the children but that he needed support. She designed an elaborate scheme to help him by having promising people from her learning groups move to live at 59 and 61 Admiral, and to be involved with the school. This scheme failed as

Malcolm became progressively more irascible and rejecting of the milieu's assistance. A woman who lived there spoke of her experience:

> "We had been carefully hand-picked by Lea to do a job, but Malcolm wouldn't allow us to do it. He permitted me to have some role in the school though for most he simply refused. I was very careful with him as he was an extremely scary man. I figured that if he disapproved of me that I could be thrown out and I didn't want to take that chance."

Malcolm had gotten one of the younger boys to leave his father and live at the school and he asked this woman to be involved in the boy's care. She welcomed him and looked after him, but it found it very difficult. Malcolm was completely in control of every detail of how she looked after the boy. If she did any slight thing he did not approve of, she would get a phone call. Malcolm expected her to clear everything through him, absolutely everything.

Over the next year, it became clear that the milieu was not working though no one wanted to say why. There was a sort of admission that Malcolm was a tyrant, but the whole focus was always on seeing what the adults living there could do to salvage the situation. There were months of painful groups with them taken by Grant or Adam. After a year or so, as Malcolm was chronically complaining to his mother, it was decided to move the intended helpers out of 59 and 61 Admiral. They moved over to 55 Admiral and started another house group. After that, the woman mentioned above had no contact with the boy she had cared for until years later when he was no longer in Malcolm's grasp. He had been told that she was his enemy. Even after the move to 55 Admiral, some connection with the school continued for another year. This limited involvement meant having regular group meetings that left the participants feeling responsible for, though unable to impact, the directions that Malcolm was imposing on them and on the school.

My own sense about Malcolm at that period is that he was not simply "languishing" as Lea would say, but that he was sinking into a profound depression with numerous characteristics of outright mental illness. As

Lea was deteriorating in the late 1970s, so was her son. The control that he had established over the children extended to their acting out his views about Therafields in general and with the people living closely with them in particular. One of the men living nearby said,

"The way the kids were allowed to talk to adults was totally objectionable. The kids were always very disdainful. That would have come from Malcolm. We were given a list of things that needed to be done at 59. One day another fellow and I went over to fix the doors. Malcolm came outside and went ballistic. I had never met him, but he was screaming at us that we had no right to be there."

Malcolm became obsessed with spotless cleanliness and safety issues. Another man told me of his first encounter with Malcolm on a Monday evening about 9:30 after one of the first milieu groups. He had gone over to 59 to visit a couple of his friends. They were with some others in a sitting area on the second floor. He heard a noise coming up the back stairs. It was Malcolm and two of the boys. He didn't know who Malcolm was. The boys had a mean look on their faces and Malcolm was furious. He began: 'You people don't seem to realize that you have a real responsibility living in a house with children and a school. I found this in the dryer and I'm not happy about it.' He then held up some fluff and went into a tirade about fire hazards and irresponsible people." The visiting fellow just stared. He thought, 'Who is this asshole?' After Malcolm threw the fluff on the floor and left, he asked the others, 'Who does he think he is?' 'Don't you know?' they asked. 'He's Malcolm Hindley-Smith.'"

Tellingly, Rob was well aware that Malcolm's stewardship of the school and the children had headed into weird and destructive territory, but out of fear of his brother and/or of confrontations with his mother and Josie, did nothing to stem that tide. Rob told me when I interviewed him in 1997 about an incident that occurred one morning when his son, Christopher was attending the school. Rob took the child over to 59 Admiral for its early morning opening at 8:30. Though a few minutes early, Rob rang the doorbell at the side door. Malcolm answered and with a manner of extreme annoyance told Rob that Christopher was not to come into the school until precisely 8:30. Soon afterwards Rob removed his son from the school but made no move to confer with other parents about the environment that Malcolm was creating. Rob told me this story, not as an expression of regret for failing to take responsibility, but almost as a joking story about how he kept his son away from Malcolm's influence.

Over time the situation with the 'supportive' milieu, Malcolm, Lea, the children and their parents, became progressively more Orwellian. Things that were true could not be spoken without fear of censure. Living in the milieu, one man found that,

> "The reality of our lives there was that everything about it
> was focused on pleasing Lea. No one took a real position
> on anything. It was impossible to raise issues about how
> things were going so long as Lea took the groups, which
> she often did. For example, no one was allowed to suggest
> that Malcolm was something of a nut-bar. It would be
> turned back as a problem of one's own."

In the Hypno I seminar, one of the therapists spoke of an incident at the school in which his son had been treated sadistically by Malcolm in front of the other kids. The details certainly bore out his conclusions. Lea said, 'Well, there's always two sides to every story.' She simply wouldn't touch it. She was trying to defend and protect Malcolm at all cost. On the other hand, she would speak about how rebellious he was and how he didn't want to have anything to do with Therafields.

Some of the interested people in the community and in the school milieu had the capacity to stick with and help individual children. If that had been encouraged and facilitated, the school would have been a great success. But a power-driven and insecure person like Malcolm was able to shut down these possibilities and make the environment impenetrable and opaque to the parents. What developed was a 'ministry of fear.' Some of the parents were badly treated and bullied by therapists who had their own agendas: not antagonizing Lea, not rocking any boats. That part of it became complex: whoever questioned anything was in trouble; there was ostracism. A lot of parents were not capable of pulling themselves out of the condition of being treated like children. One father said that,

> "In the community by this point there was a system of
> approbation and disapprobation that was absolutely as bad

as any cult that you want to describe. What had started as well intentioned and with a learning professional like Sharon, got enmeshed in a whole set of factors that were extraneous to the school, turning it into what it eventually became: Malcolm's sinecure, his playground in the worst sense."

The parents' group established in the Brunswick milieu in the early 1970s had been intended to support the many families resident there. As the relationships with the parents and Malcolm deteriorated, issues related to the school came more frequently to the fore in their meetings. The therapists taking the group were greatly influenced by Lea's determination to support Malcolm, however, and I believe that it would have been difficult to mount in any way a concerted protest about Malcolm's methods and his treatment of the parents themselves. There was never in this group a sense of safety, allowing people to talk openly about their concerns and struggles as parents. Increasingly, however, within the community, there developed talk about Malcolm and the school. Over the two or three years that I attended the seminar parents' group, I heard progressively concerned stories about Malcolm's contempt and rudeness and of his exclusion of the parents from any form of participation in the school.

In the summer of 1980, two parents of children in the school took extraordinary action to take them back from Malcolm. One successfully went to court, receiving an order from the judge that his children be 'restored' to their father. The second literally removed his son, who had been living at the school, keeping him at home until the child began to realize how he had been manipulated to turn against his parents. These actions created waves through the community. Lea called an emergency meeting. Clearly distraught by the events, Lea said something like, "Maybe we ought to just take the whole thing apart if it has come to this." Personally, I thought it sounded like a good idea, but nothing came of her suggestion. Despite this public display of resistance to Malcolm, some of the parents in the seminar group were concerned that with fewer children in the school, the already onerous fees would be higher. The man raising this concern said passionately, "We need new blood." My elder daughter was nearing school age and I was already under pressure to enrol her that fall. "Not my kid's blood," I thought. At that point, still unable to stand openly against those pressures, I chose a geographical solution. Maurice and I moved with our children to one of the houses at the farm.

Lea, Visvaldis, and the Environmental Centre

Things were quiet at the farm during much of the year and a half that we lived there. Lea was away most of the time. Visvaldis was living at the Willow with a skeleton staff. He was very depressed during the winter of 1981-2 and was drinking heavily. Trying to support him, Maurice and Philip would go over and spend time talking with him. I believe that he was suicidal. When Lea was around she seemed mostly interested in growing plants in different parts of the Willow and selling them. Since the early 1970s Lea and Visvaldis had been promoting an idea of building an 'environmental centre.' Doing so would have required a huge effort from a large group of Therafields members. It entailed buying a piece of land – Mono Centre was often cited as a possibility – and constructing housing on it. It was to include a variety of homes – separate apartments, smaller houses, and larger, shared houses. The idea was to create a long term, self-perpetuating community of people who wanted to leave the city and live communally in an emotionally and physically healthy manner. It was booted around at numerous marathons. Few attacked the idea; some discussed it with interest but absolutely nothing happened. Gone were the days of 1967 when to speak of a venture like buying a farm was to quickly see it happen. Few wanted the Centre though some continued to discuss the possibility because Lea promoted it.

Moreover, Lea and Visvaldis wanted people in the community, especially those living up north, to establish businesses under Therafields' auspices to generate income for the environmental centre. But as more people were developing independent lives, this was not happening. When one couple made their small farm-based sprout business into a separate company, Lea acted as if this was the most calculated of betrayals. Exhibiting some of the strange behaviour that was becoming more public, Lea called together a group of her loyal supporters for a "white light" session. The idea was to send 'white light' to the woman to help her to realize the error she was making. Visvaldis and Lea spoke disparagingly about people who, by working at Therafields, had developed skills, for example, in the building trades, who were then exploiting their training by working outside the community, rather than starting Therafields-based companies. They were quite indignant about this trend. Visvaldis once called the new sprout business 'a cancer on the side of Therafields.'

By the summer of 1981 there were signs that Therafields was in trouble. Aside from the things happening with Lea and Visvaldis, the organization's finances were badly compromised. Many properties had been leveraged to buy others, their rents used to pay expenses. As mortgage rates climbed in the early 80's to around 20% or more, holding all of this together became difficult. The mismanagement of the office was more obvious. Vocal seminar members continued to harass it for accountability. Finally, the seminar group decided that each therapist would work out of his or her own practice. The fees gathered would no longer go into the coffers of Therafields. This was in effect a dissolution of the company and a threat to Rob's job as administrator.

The End of Ka School

Because I had withdrawn from any possibility of my children attending Malcolm's school by moving to the farm in 1981, I learned only later the directions that life within that sphere had been taking. In 1984 Malcolm was arrested, charged, and later convicted of having had sexual relations with two under-aged girls in his charge. From the time that he took over full control of the school in 1975, Malcolm had managed to subvert the original intentions of the school to the uses of his own mental health decline, his own psychopathy. In the summer of 1977, Therafields had celebrated a fifteenth anniversary with a gala weekend at the farm and a booklet of short essays about its various aspects. The originating date was taken from the 1962 formation of the first house group, five years before the purchase of the farm and the naming of that property Therafields. One set of essays is entitled 'Education.' Sharon Healy contributed a piece outlining the history of the school from the summer of 1973. Another parent who was very involved in this process also wrote of her experiences. A third piece was written by Josie. None of these essays reflect the struggle that had already occurred, placing the care and responsibility for the children entirely in the hands of Malcolm.

Reading them now, one is taken back to those days of naiveté and group self-deception. Like all the pieces in the booklet, they are determinedly up-beat, positive promotions for the values and activities of Therafields. But in the light of what came to pass, ironies inherent to the essays are both staggering and painful. In her essay, Josie states: "Not until Malcolm Hindley-Smith got involved in the education of our children did I start to feel secure about things. I knew the welfare of the child would be his main concern. This has proved true. He has in no way countenanced the oppression of children. Since Malcolm has taken over the reins of what has been called the KA school, my own anxieties have largely come to rest. Spared conflict with parents and helpers in the running of the school, he is confident to function freely on his own intuitions, which focuses completely on the welfare of the child."

The problem with freeing Malcolm to follow his own intuitions with respect to the children was that it was precisely at that time that Malcolm was losing his grip. A strong person in charge of a school for kids can do wonderful things for them, as was witnessed in A.S. Neil's Summerhill school. But Neil was grounded and emotionally healthy in ways that Malcolm simply was not. At the beginning of his involvement with the school, Malcolm had been all energy, passion, and innovation. But by 1977 he was obviously "languishing," as Lea put it. And it was at that time when he most decisively took the reins with the children, marginalizing and stigmatizing anyone attempting to intervene. Malcolm nurtured many hatreds and took no care to shield the kids from them. On the contrary, he encouraged them to share his feelings. He hated Therafields, his mother, his sister, people who were a part of Therafields, and significantly, the children's own parents. Over the next several years, Malcolm arranged that more of the children essentially became residents at 59 Admiral, living with him in a progressively warped universe.

Once Sharon was gone, the students no longer had actual classes. They played together and went bug hunting in the yard behind the house. They were made to learn Elton John's song 'Don't Go Breaking My Heart', reciting it and singing it. They had exercise time. Each was rotated through to lead the exercises in the back yard. On the first floor was a library where Malcolm had all the Ladybug books. One could go there and read if desired, but there was never any structure. The children just went there and hung out.

Malcolm always seemed to have knowledge about personal difficulties any of the parents were experiencing. His information likely came from Lea or Josie who would have knowledge of things happening in the community, and who could be fast and easy about confidential material. Sometimes Malcolm had all the kids gather in the big room in the basement. If someone was mad at their parents, or if Malcolm simply said that he or she was, he would put pillows on the floor and say, 'Just imagine that is your parents there on the floor.' He would work that child up, getting her upset, crying, jumping up and down on the pillows, and saying, 'I hate you.' It was very conflicting because the children felt they had to keep him happy, and to make him happy they had to totally dislike their parents. If anyone didn't, she was made to feel in the wrong and he would manipulate everything she did or said to make her not want to be at home. They had to keep secrets all the time about anything they were doing at the school because if their parents knew what was happening, they would have 'broken the trust with Malcolm.' He would say, 'Your parents might take you out of the school.' He conveyed that the parents wouldn't understand his ways of doing things and that the parents were themselves bad anyway. So, the children would go home, eat dinner, go out to play, go to bed, get up and do it all over again. They were living a split life. A room on the third floor at 59 Admiral was set aside so that anyone could stay over on the weekends if they wanted. Malcolm had the children do his laundry, shovel his walk, rake the leaves, and do everything around the house.

Malcolm wasn't always around. Sometimes he would go out alone or with the two older girls and do things while the others would be there by themselves. Everyone was put into a group. Millie B (a pseudonym), who was in the school from 1973-1980 was initially with three other kids about her age and they had fun together. They would go back and forth between the back yards on Admiral and Brunswick. Millie didn't know who was in charge of them, as they were left to their own devices a lot of the time. Later Malcolm changed the groups and put Millie in one with four young girls. She was eleven then and the girls were about four or five. He told her that she was in charge and that she had to teach them. Millie remembers thinking, 'Teach them what? Who's teaching me?' She was nervous about everything she did as she knew that Malcolm would be told everything, and she was so afraid of getting in trouble.

Malcolm would pick on different people to get mad at. He would rotate it. He would pick on the boys for certain things. He picked on Millie by saying that she had no opinions on anything. Once on Canada Day everyone was going to stay over and watch the fireworks. Then Malcolm told her that she couldn't stay. She was devastated. He dragged out a table and said that she could only stay if she stood on the table and told everyone two opinions. She made up a couple of things, so he let her stay. She thought, 'What was the point of that?' Afterwards Millie had to go to his study every week and tell him three opinions. After a few weeks, he let it go.

Then he got onto someone else. He went through this with all the children. He would pick something for a few weeks and focus on one person, totally intimidating him or her. Millie was very afraid of him. She found him weird and constantly manipulative. He would scare the children, but they also wanted to please him, to stay in his good books. They would want him to invite them into the coach house or give them some special task because they would feel relieved. Malcolm thinks I'm OK so I'm OK.

In such an atmosphere, one never knew if it would be a good day or a bad day, if Malcolm would be happy with someone or with their group. To clean his car was a big favour, like a huge reward for good behaviour. He would choose someone, and that person would feel great. Then he would choose someone else and the first child would think, 'Oh, what's wrong? He doesn't think I'm good enough now.' The children never really knew where they stood. Malcolm could come suddenly upon them playing in the back yard and they wouldn't know what kind of mood he was in or if he might pick on them. When one of the kids was picked on there was nothing the others could do. Their friendships were quite strong and they all felt the same things though they would never say so. No matter who was picked on each felt badly for that kid and knew that the others felt badly for them when it was their turn. If anything was said to support the one being picked on, the speaker would be accused of something as well, so all just sat and watched. Millie recalled,

> "At the school, we had fun, but we had to grow up fast also. We learned to be careful, how to watch our backs, how to suss out a situation before we said anything or before we chose which way to go on an issue. Because if we went the wrong way, forget it. No wonder he thought I had no opinions. I had to figure out what my opinion should be before I said anything. I was very stressed being in charge of the education of the little kids. I was in charge, but I wasn't told what to do."

When one of the boys was taken out of the school by his parents in 1980, Millie remembers thinking at the time that she wished that her parents would take her out, but she would never admit that. She would go back and forth mentally between: 'I hate my parents, and, no, I don't. Malcolm's telling me that I do.' Malcolm made much about the boy who had left, telling the others how bad his parents were and how bad their parents were. He would say things like: 'You have to be careful with your parents. You can stay here. This place is safe.'

That summer someone told Millie's parents that she couldn't go to high school without a grade eight diploma, so they put her in a regular school that fall. She had to pretend that it was terrible leaving the school but part of her was relieved that she no longer had the weird scary feeling she always had around Malcolm.

> "You never knew when he was going to like you or hate you or make you feel like shit. If you were really in favour he would let you come into the coach house. He'd put his feet on your legs and say, 'You can rub my feet.' I remember thinking, 'Boy, this is big.' Now I think it was disgusting. Yes, master, it is an honour for me to rub your feet."

When she left the school, Malcolm told Millie that she could no longer play with the other children. Separation from the friends with whom she had been close for seven years was devastating. As well, being at the other school was very difficult for her in the first year. She had never sat at a desk nor done regular school work. She managed with math because Sharon had taught the times tables and some other basic things. Later they had learned the binary system and did some work on a computer. Everything else was hard for her, particularly spelling, grammar, and punctuation. Socialization was a major challenge. She had come from a place where the children just hung out and played. Suddenly, she had to deal with what group to belong to, the regular social pressures of kids. She simply didn't know how to do it.

Millie wasn't able to stay in close touch with any of the other kids after she left, though she did see one or two of them some years later. Those who stayed longer than she, couldn't stay close with each other either because when Malcom went to trial, some testified against him and some for him on the stand. That put big wedges between them. It was clear to her that many of the kids had a hard time once the school ended. It had affected many of them negatively; they came away feeling very badly about themselves.

Kerry O. (a pseudonym) was with the school from the time that it moved to the farm in 1975 until the summer of 1980. One of the five older kids, Kerry's experience differed somewhat from, but also coincided with, that of Millie. Sharon had used the formation of groups as an organizing tool, usually for activities pertinent to an age group. Kerry saw that the groups put together by Malcolm - the blue group, the peach group, and so on, were really based around the good kids and the bad kids, from a judgmental perspective.

Once the school had settled into 59 Admiral Rd, Malcolm was rarely around. He would be in the coach house. The five older students had different responsibilities, but it was mainly another girl and Kerry who ran the school. There were three women who came in to make meals. Kerry made up the schedule for them. When one would arrive, Kerry would sit with her for a bit, then send her to the kitchen to make tea. These three were the only parents that Malcolm allowed to be around. None was very secure about her position there nor about how Malcolm felt about her. Kerry would sometimes have one of them crying on her shoulder. He didn't want anyone there who was more certain of herself.

Kerry would bring the kids in when they arrived and get them settled. She collected all the fees and paid all the bills. Malcolm would come in every now and then and ask how things were going. He was obsessed with cleanliness. The place was immaculate, but he insisted on rigid cleaning schedules. There were cleaning shifts that all the children had to participate in. Kerry doesn't remember learning anything, at least in any formal way. There was no instruction. The older students would chart the progress of the younger ones through the Lady Bug books. Malcolm would appear sometimes and irritably say, 'What's going on in here'? Other times he'd be in a different mood and say, 'Let's play this fun game.' He would then talk to the kids about Einstein or something, but in the day to day running of the school, he had little to do.

Malcolm didn't want any of the other parents involved, so he manipulated things to ensure their exclusion. His would say that kids are weird when their parents are around. He would say that it was disruptive to the learning process. On reflection, Kerry wondered what all parents were thinking about. It wasn't cheap to send the children there. She knew because she looked after the finances. There were three or four terms a year and it cost about $3000/term. She would go to the bank with all the cheques, as she had signing authority. The bank clerks were nice with her, but they were curious. She was about 13 then, going to the bank in the middle of the day when she should have been in school. They had no idea what was going on.

Kerry was intimidated by Malcolm, as was everyone. He could come into the house in any kind of mood and was sometimes irrational. He would totally 'freak out' about things, for example, if there was dust on the banister. When Kerry looks back on that period now, she realizes that he was losing it, especially after he started living in the coach house. She believes that standing at one side, in some ways Malcolm had a clearer view of what was happening in Therafields. Still, he wasn't able to escape it and he lived off the fruits of it. He did see hypocrisy, sycophantic behaviour, and Lea's emerging cultic personality. But his antagonism to his mother, his sister, and what he viewed as their followers left him no constructive locations for his anger and his vision. His students took the brunt of these.

Kerry remembers his very weird mood swings though at the time she couldn't understand what was going on. He either thought a child was the best thing in the world or else he it would 'lose it' with him or her. There seemed to her no external reasons for his reactions. It was completely arbitrary. In some moods he could be great with the kids, in fact, brilliant and able to inspire. But he was abusive in many ways. Kerry reflected,

"I still wonder what people were thinking. Aside from the possibility that he might come on to young girls, did it not occur to people that it wasn't a good thing for adolescent girls to be out of touch with women from whom they could learn? Malcolm did do horrible things. Quite a few people though made him the focus for their hatred without examining their own stupidity and blindness. It was abdicating their own responsibilities. I don't mean by this to absolve Malcolm of guilt. He did what he did and he has to live with that."

Kerry believes that some of the kids were really damaged by the way that they were treated, but stresses that it wasn't just Malcolm who was hard on the kids. Certain children were isolated, consistently singled out as bad. That came from Malcolm but also from other people. In the Kendal back yard things would be said, like: 'Watch out for that kid or that group of kids. They're bad.' Other kids were seen as perfect. It's clear to her that children who passed through the school under those conditions of oppression, taught little other than to be wary of their parents and of Malcolm, utterly dependent upon Malcolm's whims and moods, made to feel that they were inherently bad or found wanting in some profound manner, could not escape unscathed.

In the microcosm of the school, there were threads and outcomes of directions that Lea was taking as early as the late 1960s in her obsession with the evils in society at large, and the necessity of intervening in the lives of families and of children in ways that ultimately brought suffering to many. As his involvement in the school had developed, Malcolm gradually asserted his position as sole decision-maker. When the school was located at 59 Admiral Rd, Lea's elaborate scheme to surround it with a milieu of her most trusted young learners, was unsuccessful. Malcolm refused to work cooperatively with them, deliberately working at antagonizing everyone. He managed to render the proffered assistance ineffective. As Lea's health declined and she was less present, her awareness of his activities also diminished. Her caretakers eventually protected her from knowledge of his state, knowing the pain and worry that it would evoke. After moving into 59 Admiral, Malcolm dropped any pretense of co-operation with the children's parents or with any Therafields associates.

Over the next years he began to live in a world peopled solely by the children over whom he developed a profound control. Freed of the society and the constraints of adults, I think that Malcolm sank deeper into a category of mental illness that had been taking him over for some time. It was characterized by irascibility, depression, megalomania, and, obsessive-compulsive and controlling features. These elements were acted out in multiple ways with the children and with any adults coming into his sphere. Through the agencies of some and passivity of many, Malcolm now had a free hand in a darkening world which contained some children of the community.

Anyone who was in a learning group, a parents' group, who supported the school, or who was in any manner an integrated part of Therafields during the 1970s and early 1980s, will recognize the patterns of the experiences of the children. In the 1970s, Lea gradually became more closed to outside influences and less able to bear dissension. She began to distinguish between those whom she could trust to support her and those who were against her. She used her considerable influence with people to get her own way and to set agendas, even framing what was to be seen as truth. Like Malcolm with the children, she could raise people up and cut them down in progressively more arbitrary ways. As Malcolm withdrew from any intervening forces, his power over the children increased but so did the depth of his disturbance. Ultimately, I think that Malcolm was acting out some version of his own childhood terrors, making himself into both the scary monster, and, the one who would be the Pied Piper, the one to protect and rescue the lost children from their evil parents.

There are many things to consider when looking at what happened to the children who attended Malcolm's school in the late 1970s and early 1980s. The events that unfolded at the school are undoubtedly the most abusive and painful experiences that occurred under the Therafields umbrella, precisely because they were experienced by children who had a right to protection and proper care. In examining the legacy of Therafields, this chapter must be faced squarely as its most heinous and shameful. We cannot simply say, "Many good things happened in Therafields and many gained from being a part of it." This is true, and those things need also to be documented and acclaimed. But like most "family" histories, there are other threads that are ignored at one's peril. What went on at the school cannot be seen as something that happened 'over there.' Rather, it was a central facet of the dynamics put in place well before its formation when Lea's focus became divided between the provision of psychotherapy and the care and fostering of her family and Visvaldis. So many distortions of original ideals and purposes had to be swallowed and acquiesced in by so many of us to allow what came to be. Issues of individual and collective responsibility need to be faced, not in order to focus blame, but in order to more deeply understand our own fallibility.

The full horror of what had been happening at the school only emerged into general consciousness when Malcolm was arrested. He engaged a woman lawyer to defend him, portraying through her the appearance of shock and innocence. His claim was that the accusations were fabricated by people from his mother's 'cult', who were determined to destroy him. A further plank of his defence was to claim that girls like to fantasize about romantic and sexual adventures and that their statements were a simple reflection of this tendency. The judge found against him, however, stating that the young women were very trustworthy witnesses. He found, moreover, that Malcolm had clearly alienated the children from their families, perversely taking control of their lives. Malcolm was sentenced to four years in prison but served only a portion of that amount in a medium security facility. Those brave young women who spoke out, stopping his reign of terror must live all their lives with the memories of what was done to them. And, there are many other stories from the school that cannot be told out of concern for the privacy of the (former) children themselves.

To write about Malcolm and the school is to look into the heart of darkness. But Malcolm by no means stands there alone. With him stand his mother, his family, her close companions and confidants, all who from early days knew the disturbances that Malcolm harboured, all who entrusted their children to him despite misgivings, all who directly or indirectly supported the school despite growing evidence of the pathology at its core, all who did not speak in an effective manner against what was happening. In sum, all of us who were a part of the community from the mid-1960s to those terrible days in the mid-1980s when the extent of Malcolm's abuse of his charges was laid bare. In this space, we all stand accused though the degrees of our responsibility lie upon a wide spectrum. Regardless of our personal locations along that spectrum, it is a painful but necessary exercise to stand there along with Malcolm. The alternative is to trust to the divisions that our society provides to protect us from positions of shame. We have categories of criminality and insanity that give us neat divides between Us and Them. Rather than leaving Malcolm alone in the shadow of evil, in all honesty, we must look upon him as a fellow human and try to understand why he took, and how he was allowed to take, the path that he followed within Therafields.

Lea and her 'Caretakers' in the Late 1970s Onward

By the mid-1970s Lea was clearly losing it, though in public she maintained the demeanour of the woman in charge. In getting his mother to basically relocate to Florida where she began to write her autobiographical novels, Rob had hoped for an unrealized 'therapeutic effect.' Over the next several years, Lea's mood swings and behaviour became more erratic. In Florida her companions would gather up the mountain of things that she had purchased that day and return them to the stores. Her phases of mania became more pronounced and she became more difficult to control. Still, no one was willing to openly declare that she was no longer fully responsible for her behaviour. Certainly, her family members and Visvaldis were incapable of asserting any authority over her. People living with her and others who visited or who were kept informed with events, remained intimidated or perhaps still in thrall with her and were unable to restrain her. Greg N, who was a part of Lea's retinue by around 1980, recalled,

> "Part of the difficulty with Lea was that even in an irrational state, she was still in charge. People were treating her as sane even though she was crazy, so a lot of the damage that she inflicted on herself continued."

Lea had preached an anti-medical-model position from the late 1960s. Earlier she had been proud to state that her uncle had been a doctor. She also claimed to have received some training as a nurse at Great Ormond St Hospital. Influenced by the writing of Robert Lindner who railed against conformity, and likely because of her own insecurity about education and credentials, she gradually became more disdainful of medical, especially psychiatric, approaches. It would have required an enormous paradigm shift for Lea to view and acknowledge her problems as being those of mental illness. Her father's incarceration and death in a mental hospital had been traumatizing for her, a frightening and painful memory. No one of her students, family, or retinue had studied what is called in that literature, abnormal psychology. Thus, it was never possible to have a dispassionate look at the bipolar condition which was more and more taking her over. Earlier Lea in many ways had drawn power from rising up above her depression, likely assisted by 'uppers,' --- medication that she was able to get through the two doctors who were part of Therafields in those days. Later, she became more and more obsessive in her activities, especially her health activities. She would fast with intensity. She was always going for a powerful 'solution', not recognizing that those experiences were wearing out her physical body as well.

Glenda, another of Lea's caregivers in the late 1970s, had been one of her clients in her early days in therapy, but when Lea left for North Carolina in 1968, she was passed on to another therapist along with about 80 others. She had only two meetings with him as he was entirely overloaded. When Lea returned, Glenda's transference to her as her grandmother took over in full force.

> "It wasn't just, she reminds me of my grandmother; it was: she IS my grandmother. My grandmother had raised me a lot; she was a sort of mother to me. As a kid, I saw my job to be her pal, to help her, to cheer her up. I then became that for Lea for years. My therapy stopped at that point. I had other good and bad experiences but that was the real end of my therapy. It was an on-going transference that was never worked with; it was just taken for cash."

By 1978-9 Glenda realized that things were not right with Lea. The kind of blaming that went on within the small inner group of caretakers and family had become rampant. On one occasion Lea broke a bone. There was a barrage about how everyone was to blame for it. But even before that incident, Glenda experienced terrible manipulations by Lea, gathering people to go against one other. Once in Florida, she was made the brunt of such an attack. Lea was insecure about her relationship with Visvaldis. Barrie and Marie spearheaded an accusation that Glenda was flirting with Visvaldis, though she wasn't attracted to him at all. For a couple of days, Glenda was completely reeling from the attack. It took her that long to realize that Lea was behind it, though she hadn't make the accusation herself. Glenda believed that Barrie was generally a good guy, but she also saw his susceptibility to be used by Lea as a battering ram. Lea would gather a group of people together if there was something she wanted to get done, or something she wanted out of a situation. She would then gather the energy and force of the group by speaking passionately about the issue. Afterwards, various people would be dispatched to do what was needed. They were the designated 'executioners.' They would do what was needed as though it came from their own feelings.

In late 1979, early 1980, the Florida household was chaotic. Glenda spoke of people getting drunk, having affairs, jumping in and out of bed with one another.

> "It was a madhouse; it was wild. This one was drunk under the bed; this one was coming home drunk, though these things were not spoken of directly. Visvaldis was 'a baby dill pickle.'"

A great deal of information about people was shared openly. Lea would tell Josie things that would happen in groups or about things people had told her. There was no confidentiality. To travel with Lea, Glenda had given up teaching and working with clients. She was massaging Lea and was at her beck and call 24/7.

Being with Lea then meant giving up one's life and one's life's blood for the cause. If you didn't go along, Lea would turn on you. Life within that circle then seemed to Glenda like growing up in a really tough extended family where the big thing was squabbling over the mother's affection. There was lots of sibling rivalry. Still, she believed that she could grow strong if she could deal with it, fend for herself, and at the same time develop friendships. Glenda saw that Lea had never resolved her own sibling rivalry. She saw her setting people up, bringing them along as strong people and then knocking them down. She didn't want anyone to achieve real parity with herself. Her kids weren't real friends with each other. That seemed to Glenda to be the real resolution within any family:

> "all the crap fades, and friendship takes over. The other stuff isn't important anymore. Where the mother is the centre and the kids are vying with one another, hooking up one by one with her, everyone is simply a spoke to her wheel. Lea couldn't be equal to anyone else – not her children, not her colleagues. There was never an equal colleague."

Late in 1979, Glenda began to pull back from Lea. The group had been in Florida, then Hawaii, then back to Florida. Glenda was realizing more and more that she had no life of her own. She thought, "'This is crazy.' I knew that if I was going to make a change that I'd have to put up with all the shit and the flak and the blackballing that would come my way." Though Lea resisted her move, Glenda went to stay at the farm for the winter of 1979-80, taking care of the Willow. While there, her father died rather suddenly. She called Florida to tell people what had happened but there was no response at all. She viewed it as the way that Lea and the family had behaved when Harry died: when a real human need arose, they didn't respond from their hearts. Glenda was looked at then as a kind of bad guy for not being in Florida with Lea. The sheer lack of friendship amazed her. After that Glenda no longer lived with Lea or travelled with her.

Greg N was living in Florida at that time, as the caretaker of the two houses. He had come into therapy around 1970 and had followed the routine of taking psychological tests, going to a team of learning CAG therapists, entering a group founded by Lea for the clients of the new learners, entering a house group, and later the Gemini learning group. In retrospect he found that

> "the therapy was fairly poor, all of it. Gemini was pretty much a waste of time for everyone. The dynamic was not

well understood. On the other hand, it was facilitated as well as it could be at that historical period. In terms of what was available then, it was OK. My own therapists were not especially good, and the group therapists were in over their heads, but they were all fairly compassionate."

What Greg found most helpful was working at the farm and wrestling with his relationships there. He got interested in different aspects of therapy and picked up what he could from different teachers within and outside the community. By the mid-70s, he could see that things were becoming unravelled, that there was lots of activity but without much purpose. The centre, the focus, was weak. By then he was living at the farm and though he could see some things clearly, he was still caught up in it, still thinking that it was possible for things to heal. But when he sat in on the seminar groups, he could sense the intense turmoil under the surface that was not being dealt with. As he became more involved with Lea and her family, Greg came to understand that there was a dynamic that was influencing everything in the community. He believed that people were intimidated by her, but they also were in a hypnotic, transference kind of trance, a dream scenario something like sleep walking.

Greg gradually became even more involved with Lea and her family while living in Florida. When Glenda left in late 1979, he became her replacement, travelling with Lea, giving her massages and caring for other details of her daily life and her environment. He spoke of the problems during this period.

"The group moved back and forth between Florida and Canada and later went for awhile to Arizona. During the next two years, Lea's mental and emotional decline coincided with a lot of self-healing she was trying to do with fasting. Periodically she suffered severe electrolyte imbalance. Eventually she went over the edge into a breakdown. She had done too much damage for her body and mind to recuperate. That's when things began to deteriorate. She was doing more and more things that were hurting her. She got involved with some dentist, and she was also seeing a naturopath. By then she had acquired the Palace Pier apartments. Things had broken down severely for her and they declined over the next couple of years to a really bad state. But still no one stepped in. Her force and power were such that little could be done. A lot of people did try to help her but there was no access. Things degenerated. After the group returned from Arizona, there was a team of three or four taking care of her. Visvaldis was around but he couldn't handle her breakdown. He was falling apart himself and was drinking heavily. For a while, different members of her retinue were on 24 hour shifts with her. She had a lot of trouble sleeping; someone had to be constantly with her."

Greg found working for Lea during that period of her decline a curious experience, like living in an enclosed capsule. He didn't know much of what was happening in the community. But when he came back to it round 1981-2, he could see that it was falling apart the same way Lea was. Dissatisfaction had continued to surface among members of the seminar. Rob and Barry were struggling to keep things together, but it seemed more and more that they would not be able to do so. Conversations about the directions of, and especially about the finances of Therafields, never seemed resolved.

A lot of the people who had been attracted to Therafields to do their own therapy work had not gained a well-developed sense of themselves. Some who came for help found that what sense of self they did have got taken over and submerged in the needs of Lea and/or the 'community.' At the end they were left asking, "What happened to the promise?" Greg believes that many had grown and developed but found it hard to say if it was because of, or in spite of, what they experienced.

He saw that at the core of Therafields, an upper-class system had evolved, especially for those close to Lea. One could be a servant, but also sort of a part of the family, a familiar with the secrets. A lot of people got drawn into those roles because of their own existing family patterns that they had been trying to escape. At the same time, Greg believes that there was a good component to all of this. Anyone close to Lea's family, for that matter all the therapists, had some background of a calling to serve. What everyone needed was help to balance and control how much they would do of service and how much should have gone into developing lives of their own. The really bad thing that happened to all the underlings was that the desire to be of service was taken over and made into a personal service. Some very decent people were drawn in and were used to ends that later they regretted.

The politics of the situation could never be openly addressed. Where there are power differentials, there is politics whether you want it or not. Lea was good at sorting out the problems of individuals but not at sorting out the politics. She had a gut instinct as a power broker – how to manipulate to get what she wanted and needed, and how to massage people this way and that way verbally and make them acquiesce. But she could not, or would not, look at the politics. So that side of things didn't get put through an analytical cleansing filter. The system was really a patriarchy but there was no acknowledgement that there were other ways of dealing with a community. We did not look at things from a feminist or democratic perspective. Other approaches that might have given her and others a more critical perspective weren't allowed. People who advocated a political analysis, were systematically shut down.

When interviewing Greg, I asked if he had felt any of the sense that others had spoken of about being close to the "Royal Family" when working with Lea. "Oh, yes," he answered.

> "The whole aspect of it as the royal family was real. The dispensing of favours and attention was like that. But it was a dysfunctional family. Some people were labelled black sheep; others were the chosen ones. Some would move back and forth in those places. For a while, one person would be the good one; then he or she'd fall from grace and someone else would be the good one."

Within the larger community too Lea had her favourites. Greg noticed the way that they formed an inner group and stuck together. He was also aware of her attraction to people with a streak of psychopathy. For some reason she really liked them and liked to have them around her. They were the people she would often talk to or call upon in a group and give weight to what they said, mostly because they would be supportive of her, or else they would keep quiet when they didn't agree with her, or if they knew secrets that she did not want revealed. He confirmed Glenda's experience of how some could become her "point" people, there to support the status quo or to go after someone who challenged it.

Like most of us, while immersed in the ambience of Lea and her family, Greg was involved in a lot of self-deception: he would see things and would then ignore them. He would struggle to make sense of things but always with Lea in the right. A lot of the reason that he had ended up at the centre of things was that he drove himself there out of insecurity. As Lea deteriorated and drew him closer, he recognized that he was afraid to let go. He had a part in keeping things going, even if he didn't see himself as a powerful player in what was happening. He experienced himself more as an observer. Lea and he had a few run-ins but there was never an equal exchange. If there was a disagreement, he would be 'therapized' by Lea and the others until he came into line. In the beginning, he would see any issue as his problem. But as Lea started to weaken, he began to wake up and to feel more clearly all the things that he had seen. He believes that to some extent he may have woken up sooner than others because he was right beside her. It was madness that he saw, though he continued to see people treating her as if she was sane. When she began to break down, Greg found his distance.

Despite Lea's control over her environment and her caretakers, she did at times allow herself to be vulnerable and to surrender herself to others, but in such a way that nothing substantial could come of it. When this happened with some of the people who were looking after her, not one of them was in a position to give her any boundaries. She could not be confronted. If one did so in a diplomatic way, she might fly off the handle but later consider what had been said and act on it – though she would never acknowledge that she was taking that person's advice.

Being so close to Lea over the years, people of her entourage saw a lot of her foibles and excesses. She was a woman with considerable emotional baggage but also enormous strengths. In some ways they were in positions to have a more balanced view of her than others had. As years went on though, Meg, for example, became more bothered by her eccentricities and egocentricity. In the early days, Lea was not so much affected by people's praise of her work. Later though she needed it. It's an occupational hazard. There are a lot of therapists whose strongest suit is not the way they deal with negative feelings. These are not pleasant and some of the negative feelings that came Lea's way were very intense.

Toward the End

In 1981, Dan went up to the Willow and found Visvaldis in an alcoholic state. He had been drunk for about six or eight weeks. Lea was going to Florida and Visvaldis went as well. When Dan followed soon afterwards, he couldn't believe the things that were going on. It was "utter craziness and chaos. The team taking care of Lea was going through hell." When Lea really collapsed and required more care, Rob appealed to the seminar to support her financially, but most were unresponsive. By then figures had been made available about the on-going costs of Lea's entourage. Visvaldis returned to Toronto with Dan and lived with him for awhile. He was in a breakdown state and was suicidal. He told Dan that he had had only about six weeks of sessions with Lea, so he never really had therapy and he was never given any boundaries. He wasn't working at architecture; he had no job; Lea had simply created things for him to do.

Amazingly, it was at exactly this period that an elaborate plan was developed and proposed to establish a health centre at the farm under the leadership of Lea and Visvaldis. In March 1982 R. J. Long Consulting Limited submitted an undoubtedly expensive report of about 75 pages to the administration. The submission included a review of planning documents, an aerial site reconnaissance, discussions with approval agencies, and meetings with the Niagara Escarpment Commission staff and Mono Township officials. A municipal planning expert had been retained. His report was included.

The proposal was to build a facility on Therafields property north of Side Road #5 – likely using the Capricorn farm land as it stands at the highest point, providing the excellent eastern view mentioned in the report. The facility would allow for up to 70 people to come for a two week stay 'to devote themselves to recovering their health.' It envisioned three dining rooms, places for exercise, bedrooms, laboratories for research, preparation rooms, staff rooms, maintenance shops, and lots of parking. The Willow seems to have been included as a site for clients. It was listed as a mansion of over 10,000 square feet.

As Therafields was then heading toward bankruptcy, one can only wonder what those involved in this expensive foray into fantasy (primarily Rob and Rik) were thinking. The documents included information about the ownership of the properties. According to deeds accessed by the consultant, Rik Day had purchased the Phoenix farm from 'Mr. and Mrs. Sullivan' in 1979. Tom and Josie had somehow become owners of that property though others had been investors. The existence of an earlier verbal agreement about shares was denied by Rob and Rik. Rob alone was listed as the owner of the Schoolhouse property across the road from the Willow. These are other examples of the way that properties acquired by Therafields or by others for use by Therafields found their way into the pockets of Lea or her family.

While Lea was living at the Palace Pier in 1982 she had several people taking care of her. Glenda went once to visit and asked where she was. Someone said that she had been sleeping for about a day and a half. She had hit her head in the bathroom and the crew thought that she needed sleep. Glenda tried to wake her but was unsuccessful. Lea hadn't been up to the bathroom and had nothing to drink so was very dehydrated. Glenda called Stan and got a nurse to come over. Glenda believed that Lea would have died. She had been quiet, so people decided to just leave her. Glenda raised 'blue murder' over the episode with the on-site team and with Lea's family. She insisted that there be a medical presence. Lea's caretakers were well meaning but were not qualified for what was happening. Afterwards, those involved tried to find a retirement home for her. She did go to one place, but the administration wouldn't keep her because she was so outrageous.

In 1982-3 Lea suffered an outright psychotic period and was hospitalized. A few days earlier, Meg had gone up to the Willow to see her. Before she left the city, Stella had called Meg to tell her that Lea was 'going through something strange.' She had been up since 5AM and they were trying to keep her calm. When she arrived, Meg found that Lea was like a little girl, totally distracted in a manic state, not recognizing anyone very well. While in this state Lea would tell people that she was the Queen of England, achieving in her delusion the elite status that she had wanted for herself and her family. After her breakdown, Meg saw that Lea was not at all the same: all the charisma and the leadership ability were gone. She was simply an ordinary, older woman.

Though diagnosed with a psychosis triggered by her bipolar condition, many people around her could not stomach the idea that this was the cause of her condition. Over a decade later, one of the therapists was furious with me when I mentioned her state during that period. He clearly believed that to say Lea suffered from a manic-depressive condition was to insult her. To acknowledge a mental health issue in an important other was to stigmatize them. It was part of Lea's own legacy of anti-medical theory and practice. Ironically, it prevented her from receiving help at an earlier stage when her health might have been salvaged and her life been more productive and happy.

When Lea was hospitalized, Visvaldis was sent back to his mother and his sister to be looked after. Later that year, he committed suicide by jumping from the balcony of his apartment. After her release from the hospital, Lea lived in a house on Walmer Rd with one of her former colleagues. They had a housekeeper, though it was difficult to keep anyone for long as Lea could be so demanding. Glenda came one last time to see her in 1984. It was clear to her that for at least five years, the care of Lea had been foisted on anyone who could be controlled or shamed into it. Her family never came together to say: this is our mother; we should look after her now in her old age.

During the years that Lea was losing her grip on reality, she didn't understand what was happening to her and no one involved with her was able to diagnosis her condition. People whom she consulted, like her naturopath, were often taken with her. She could be charming and brilliant. People like him would listen to her talk about how her troubles manifested themselves in her body. She would speak of her mood swings as related to hypoglycemia rather than connecting them to mental health issues. Over time, she deteriorated more and more. After her hospitalization, even on her good days, people who visited found that she wasn't very coherent. She would come in and of out of a haze. She constantly wanted in those days to be reinstated as the head of Therafields.

The year that Dan was president of the corporation, he didn't spend much time with her because he experienced it as an assault. She would say, "Let me back; let me do it." She thought her work, her mission, wasn't finished, that there were incomplete areas that she wanted to do with the therapists. But Dan believed that what she missed was power. A year or so after Visvaldis died, Lea was becoming somewhat clearer. She then asked Dan why Visvaldis didn't come to see her, so he told her that he had died and how he had died. Lea became upset about how things had gone generally in Therafields and in her personal life. Dan consoled her, saying that she should take credit for bringing some people to an awareness of wanting to be therapists. When Lea died in 1987, it was more or less a non-event in the former Therafields community. Glenda remembered how at the Centre offices, she overheard Adam casually telling Tom, "Oh, Lea died last night." Few attended Lea's funeral other than her immediate family.

The Dissolution
of Therafields

There was never a formal breaking-up of the community of Therafields. Rather, during the 1980s its denouement came about gradually, happening in various ways for different people. The discontent about the lack of financial accounting that had surfaced in 1975 continued as a backdrop within the seminar into the early 1980s. A promised 'reveal' never occurred, but the issue stoked a growing divide between the working therapists and the administration. As Lea's sanity, presence, and influence waned, demands strengthened for a serious change of direction, leading to the therapists' claiming their own private practices in 1981.

Another precipitating force necessitating change was the steep rise of mortgage rates in 1981-2 into the 20% area. Properties had been mortgaged to the max to allow for new purchases. With interest inflation, the income no longer supported the expense of running them. Even though there were cut-backs, it was necessary to begin selling off properties. The working therapists who used the Centre offices feared that everything would be sold and that there would be no place for them to practice therapy. In this period, there were two attempts to dislodge Rob as administrator. One was a signed petition that was put together by several of the therapists while at a meeting at Grant's home. It was given to Lea and to Barrie, but it was unsuccessful, in part because of the lack of consistent pressure exerted by the cabal of signers, but also because of the inability Lea, Rob, and Barrie had in facing the reality of the situation.

Later it became clear that Therafields was going bankrupt. About $50,000-$100,000 was needed to prevent foreclosure by the bank. Money was raised among some of the therapists as shares. In no uncertain terms, one condition of their doing so was that Rob would resign and that the shareholders would take over the company. What was left then was the Centre (316, 318, 320 Dupont), a few houses, the farm, and the Willow. The latter were sold off and only the Centre remained. Rob simply wasn't a good businessman and as Dan stated, there is the possibility that he was using the corporation's money as a sacred cow, milking it for himself. This was never categorically said, and no one ever went through the books with an intent to prove it. However, many thought that if one looked at Rob's life-style, the way he was living given his salary, one might ask 'What else was he paying himself?' Over the years, Rob's refusal to give a transparent accounting of the finances of the company had engendered considerable suspicion.

At the same time, those close to the situation didn't believe that Barrie was involved with financial discrepancies. In 1981, Barrie voluntarily gave up his position and salary as the vice-president of Therafields. His concern at the time was that the organization honour its commitment to redeem the shares of those who had contributed to its development but who were now moving on. The loss of this income placed him in a financially precarious position for the next several years. Barrie's problem seemed to be more that his tie to Lea made it difficult for him face up to the reality of what was happening both with her and within the larger picture. He was distancing himself from his central involvement in the running of Therafields with Rob and Rik, however, finding directions they were taking disappointing.

I moved on from Therafields in the summer of 1983 after the end of my marriage and with my immersion in academic life. I had attended a few seminar meetings in the fall of 1982 after we returned from the farm. One of the men who had been periodically close to Lea was promoting an idea of using the seminars to allow each person to speak at length about his or her experience of Therafields. As in an AA meeting, there was to be no cross talk. Each was to have a space to talk without fear of criticism or confrontation. His hope was to develop some consensus about the path that we had trodden together over the past 15-20 years, possibly leading to some new vision of the future. In the event, however, little was accomplished. Too many people were ready to simply move on; too many unresolved grievances had never and would never see the light. In the seminar, individual power struggles had broken out and factions were forming. As various people began to get their own sense of what had been happening, some became angry, beginning to throw their own perceptions into the mix. Many found the meetings painful. They had already had enough. Gradually the seminar simply ceased to meet.

With the sale of the houses, most house groups came to an end, but by then many of the members were moving on anyway. People who had come into therapy 10 or more years previously in their youth, were now more interested in their own personal lives. There was a positive rash of marriages and the having of children in that era. Most members of the community had always had jobs and careers outside Therafields. But a few who had been in Lea's later "learning groups," sought other sites of learning and became therapists in their own right. Others who had developed skills such as various aspects of construction and carpentry while on Therafields' work sites, began their own companies.

I went to see Lea in early 1984 at her home on Walmer Road up past Casa Loma. I was engaged in undergraduate psychology courses and had heard that Lea wanted to sell her books. She had a complete set of Freud's volumes that I wanted to buy. Meeting her there in her new residence, both of us in entirely new phases of our lives, was unlike any previous interaction. My early encounters with her on Admiral Rd had been wonderful. They had opened to me the possibilities of community and of learning about myself and of others at quite a deep level. As she had moved away from her practice and become more of a figurehead, she became for me a larger-than-life personage, at once compelling and a threat. At the Walmer Rd house, we met as an early middle-aged woman embarking on a new career, and, an older woman, essentially finished with the centrally commanding location that had been hers. She was keen to see me. We chatted at some length about the end of my marriage. She was interested in all the details. She didn't ask about my studies or the directions I was taking. She seemed lonely, anxious to visit and to hear whatever interesting gossip I might bring. It was the last time I was to see her.

At this remove of over thirty years, I am more able to feel compassion for and an understanding of Lea. She had learned early the lesson that there were details of one's life and inner self that would be revealed to others at great peril. The creation of a face with which to interact with 'the other,' and, the suppression and denial of any pieces that could bring opprobrium, were essential to success in daily life. But over time, the energy needed to maintain these divisions cannot be sustained. The ultimate wreckage of Lea's life, family, and therapeutic project was the result. I have developed a sense of compassion for the young woman who was Lea, endeavouring to find a way in her life that was of value to herself, her family, and to the clients and students whom she had taken on. Hobbled by her need to deny the actual conditions of her own early life, she perforce had to dissemble and lie increasingly not just to others but to herself as well. And it destroyed the best that was in her. A Grecian tragedy in several acts.

Conclusion

During the 1950s, Lea Hindley Smith found her way into what later became for her a substantial psychotherapy practice. The beginnings were humble enough. A talent for reading cards and tea leaves, likely learned while she lived as a young woman in England, became an entry into counselling individuals impressed by her insights and practical wisdom. She read widely in psycho-analytic literature, primarily the works of Freud, identifying herself as one of those whom he had foreseen becoming 'lay analysts,' that is, therapists without a medical degree. Her year or so of therapy with a member of the British Psychoanalytic Society and the technique of hypnosis taught to her when she lived in Yorkshire during the war, sketched general patterns of procedure while she felt her way along.

As her clientele grew she began to see those who came to her in groups as well as individually. In sessions or in groups people would speak of their troubles and Lea would help each to understand more deeply the origins of their problems, most often related as they were to experiences within his or her family of origin. With this knowledge, and with support and encouragement, many of her clients gained from their work with her and moved on into other aspects of their lives. Bringing some of her clients to live in houses owned by her, sometimes alongside her and her family, Lea moved into wholly new territory. The intimacy and intensity of the relationships developed in house groups by members with one another and with Lea, initiated a climate from which one did not lightly move on. Communal life, friendships, the excitement of new learning, the potential for mating, militated against any notion of simply doing one's therapy and moving off. To where? To suburbia? To a life like that of our parents?

When Father Gregory Baum and his students came into Lea's sphere in 1964, all of the components above were already in place. Over the next two years, as these new clients, soon learners, and the others whom they referred to her entered her groups and newly-founded house groups, Lea's practice spiralled to unworkable hundreds. John N who had been working with her for some time believes that at that moment the entire community would have benefited had Lea stopped what had been an almost automatic inclusion of anyone who came to see her. He was aware that many, or possibly most of the members of the Hypnotherapy learning group, were not sufficiently grounded in their own therapy to start to work with people. They needed a longer incubation period with Lea than she could then give to them. In fact, personal therapy ceased for most by 1967-8 after the Bigwin marathon because of the pressure to prepare the farm as a site for group marathons. When Lea left for North Carolina soon after, they had to take over, and then ultimately retain, the bulk of Lea's individual practice and groups. On her return, Lea was no longer available to them in ways that had been the signature climate of her practice – a woman open to accepting of all and every form of emotion as material to be understood, normalized, and resolved; a woman who bravely went toward her work with all comers to be of help to them, to release them, as she would say, 'to their glorious selves.'

Lea's determination to live a different kind of life than she had had transformed her relationship with the community that her work had engendered. The very power of the therapeutic work done on the marathon at Bigwin Island in the summer of 1967 had overwhelmed her already taxed physical and emotional resources. When she returned to Toronto in early 1968 after being treated at Duke University for type-2 diabetes, she ventured into areas that puzzled and troubled some of the fledgling therapists who had until then felt closely aligned with her. She began a sexual relationship with the husband of one of her clients, formulating a theoretical perspective of her own to explain and justify her behaviour, and, aggressively challenging and humiliating any of her former students who were unhappy with her. To all intents and purposes, she withdrew from the purposeful therapeutic work that had been her staple, establishing herself rather as the centre of a kind of learning that over several years became less and less relevant. Unable to examine her own early traumas or the guilt that she carried about relations with her children, Lea had more and more to hide from herself and from others.

The underlying core of her attention became self-protection, the care and feeding of her lover Visvaldis, and of her children. Accomplishing these goals meant the subversion of many of the core tenets of Lea's earlier practice. Listening to and falling in line with Visvaldis' interests and vision, she elevated the physical labour needed to prepare the farm for marathon work into an essential, even a necessary aspect of the community. With Rob, Barrie, and Rik at the helm, various financial sleights-of-hand regarding properties and salaries gradually benefited the entire family. Josie, with no real therapy or training, became a well-paid 'therapist,' a role, I would contend that she never understood. Nonetheless, she mined this position for over a decade to get help with her children, care of her homes, massage, and in one case, a lover.

But the most damaging fallout from Lea's relentless use of Therafields resources was the wreckage left behind of the promising Montessori school begun by Sharon Healy. With the compliance of Josie and a few other allies, Lea engineered the complete take over of the school by her son, Malcolm. From 1975, when this was accomplished until 1984 when Malcolm was arrested and later convicted of the sexual abuse of two of his minor students, an ever-darkening sense of the school and of Malcolm pushed its way into the communal consciousness. Lea and her allies adamantly refused any questioning of his role and methods. Children and their families have borne the brunt even into the present day of her need to stand by her son.

By at least early 1975, people close to Lea recognized behaviours and ideas emerging that perplexed them. Rather than acknowledging the fact that she was in trouble, her son Rob erected another layer of public obfuscation. He pushed her into moving for long periods to the houses that had been purchased near Clearwater, Florida for holiday and marathon uses. She was given, and happily took up, the task of writing stories that became a series of autobiographical novels, soon foisted on the community as the literature of the century. Her new job did not provide the therapeutic solution that Rob had hoped for. However, it did prevent quicker recognition in the community as a whole that Lea was gradually descending into progressively more disturbed and irrational states.

With her lessened involvement in the seminar, discontent below the surface emerged full blown in the summer marathon of 1975. During that year, the numbers of people seeking therapy had dropped. But the cost of administering all of the assets of Therafields – the farm, the Willow, other rural properties, the offices on Dupont Ave., and the dozens of house groups -- had ballooned. The administrators – Rob, Barry, and Rik were attempting to raise money by changing the fees system that had long been in place. Rather than charging a common rate for sessions, groups, and house group rental, each client was to pay a flat monthly fee based on his or her income, regardless of the numbers of sessions or groups attended. The new schedule was creating waves in the community; many were unhappy with the new charges. At the same time, therapists who had been working hard in the trenches for almost ten years, who through their work were producing the bulk of the income, felt frustrated with their own stagnant pay rates and, in particular, with the lack of financial accountability to them of the administration.

Tensions between the administration and a core group of the therapists grew apace. By 1980 there had been two attempts to unseat those in charge. Barrie had by then withdrawn from his salaried position, working more intensely in the arts community of which he had long been a part. In 1981, the therapists voted to establish practices of their own, ending the arrangements under which they had submitted all fees to the administration and received a salary. With the escalation of interest rates, Therafields holdings became vulnerable.

There was a veritable fire sale of the houses, some bought by people living in them, some by the therapists. Therafields was close to bankruptcy. It was rescued by a group of the therapists, concerned about maintaining the Centre on Dupont as their offices, who agreed to raise the money needed to keep it afloat, on condition that Rob give up his position as the administrator.

The seminar continued to meet for another year or so, mainly dealing with issues relating to the administering of the corporation. An attempt to give a forum to seminar members for a collective reflection on their experiences floundered when disagreements about the past made the sessions contentious. From 1983-85 two groups met periodically to discuss setting up a training school for therapists, especially to help people who had been part of one of Lea's later learning groups and who wanted to become psychotherapists. By 1985, the groups had amalgamated and founded the Centre for Training in Psychotherapy, a respected school which to this day graduates students who are registered in the new Ontario College of Psychotherapists.

By the late 1970s, Lea's mental and physical health had precipitously deteriorated. People travelling with her gradually were shifted into custodial care. After her period of hospitalization, Lea never regained her early power and charisma. She lived the remainder her life relatively quietly, dying at the age of 76 in 1987.

The rise and dissolution of Therafields is a classic tale of people falling in love with a charismatic leader and cleaving to her despite developing signs that she herself had lost her moorings. The outcomes were tragic for some. People who had worked with Lea, who loved her and owed a great deal to her and who were committed to being a part of the community that had formed around her, became divided within themselves in the same way that she was divided. It was certainly not the case that no one saw that the emperor had no clothes. Individuals had pushed against particular trends or enactments over the years, but because there was no collective movement, for example, within the seminar, it could not be said in an effective manner:

> "Lea has made some bad decisions and is not being open or honest about them. This is not working; we have to acknowledge that fact and so does Lea; we have to get back to basics and see what we are about."

Others needed to come forward to carry on not just her work but her leadership. There were people who had the capacity for doing just that. Why this did not happen both early on and much later in the history of Therafields involves all the usual sources of human failures to which we are subject.

The core had changed, but that fact could not be acknowledged. Too much was invested in the way things had been, both for Lea and for us. We didn't have the perspective to see her as one of a possible number of teachers who could help to give direction to our lives. We couldn't, as a nascent community, accept her fallibility. It is my belief that all of us who in one location or another failed to critically evaluate and mount effective counter measures to some of the patently destructive currents that emerged, stand to some degree responsible for these along with Lea and her children.

My own experiences in Therafields were the most important formative elements of my young adulthood. I remain grateful to Lea for taking me into her practice, for the many things I learned from her, and particularly for giving me a path toward my own life as a psychotherapist.

Epilogue 1: Another Look at Intentional Communities of the 1960s and 1970s

By the end of the 1960s some of political agitation among American young people was eased. The assassinations of inspirational leaders: JFK, Martin Luther King, Robert Kennedy, Medgar Evers, and Malcolm X, had dealt heavy blows to idealism and the hope for a better future. A new spirit of cynicism – get what you can; manipulate and win at all cost, was more evident. A serious downturn in the economy in the mid-1970s left many communities vulnerable and unable to continue. Members left their communities with the sense that it was time for them to move on and to make use of what they had learned – for some this resulted from simply growing older, possibly more mature. Many communities did continue after the 1960s and 1970s – hundreds, particularly those based on spiritual principles, were still functioning in the USA at the turn of the millennium. Some changed directions and conditions successfully. Communities in which members lived closely with one another were less likely to survive than those that allowed greater personal and familial privacy.

In interviews done in 1995 with Americans who had lived communally in the 60s and 70s, Timothy Miller and his co-workers found that they continued to have largely fond memories of the life. Fewer than a half dozen of the hundreds of members or former members refused to be interviewed. Generally, there was great enthusiasm for the experience in their lives and for that moment in American life. Some had found its intensity exhausting, but more often it was described as exhilarating and life-changing. Asked if their communal lives had been a failure, few said that it was, even if it had been difficult and chaotic. Most found it to have been a valuable learning experience, even if the community itself had not survived. Interviewers found that most former community members had carried on the values they had embraced in their communal lives by becoming good parents, responsible citizens, and by doing work of social value: teaching, social work, health food or organic vegetable providers, artists, nuns and priests, small business owners, and so on.

These responses are consistent with most of those that I received when interviewing former Therafields members in 1997-8. I did, however, meet with other responses. There were people who did not want to be interviewed for reasons of personal privacy or because of anger they held toward Lea, Malcolm, and other members of the community, especially because of the way that their children had been harmed.

And, how did the kids fare? In the communes that Miller explored, children were not always closely supervised and there were hazards whether in rural or urban settings. Generally, he found that parents who raised their children communally, and the kids themselves, were happy about their experiences and the ways that they turned out. (pg. 239) Many children raised during the central years of the Therafields experience recall that period with fondness. They had childhood friends and adult caretakers who are like extended family to them now. The families, parents, and children who met with interference by Lea, or who were significantly harmed by their connection with Malcolm and his school, maintain angry, even bitter memories of ways that they were treated, not simply by Lea and Malcolm, but by those who dismissed their concerns about the children and the school at the time that the damage was being done.

There has never been any reckoning about these issues, no forum of truth and reconciliation that could in some manner address the wounds so inflicted. When the community essentially disbanded in early to mid-1980, people went their own ways, carrying their gains and losses into the next stages of their lives. No central leadership remained or evolved that could pull together an effort to understand or deal with the residues of the preceding era.

Epilogue 2: Another Communal Example, Another Cautionary Tale

While working on my Therafields blog, I read Michael Downing's book, *Shoes Outside the Door*. To me it is example of another intentional community of the same period that had shared many elements, both wholesome and troubling, with Therafields. Downing wrote about problems in the Zen Centre in San Francisco that came to a head in 1983 and led to the forced resignation of the abbot, Richard Baker. There is much in Browning's account that bears resemblance to the dynamics in Therafields that ultimately led to its succession of crises and its dissolution about this same period. There are many important differences as well, but it is instructive to look at another community formed in the 1960s, with a practice at its core – in this case 'zazen', the study of self through meditation and mindfulness, and with charismatic leadership that later went awry, confusing and dividing the core members – not just with one another, but within themselves as well.

The responses that long-time members gave about their feelings toward the Zen Buddhist priest, Suzuki-Hiroshima who came from Japan in 1959, gradually founding a Zen Centre, read very like those given by people who knew and were involved with Lea in the early days when her practice was the true and dynamic centre of her life. People said: "I loved him; he was my teacher, my friend; I felt that he saw me and accepted me to the depths." "I wanted to be around him, there was peace with him; I'd go with some neurotic problem and in ten minutes it didn't seem like a problem any more. The words would just fall out of my mouth like a pool on the floor and all I would want to do is to be with this beautiful man;" "I loved Suzuki-Hiroshima: he was the most important influence in my life." "We were his students; he loved us; he would have died for us; he was devoted to us." "He taught me to trust." A man who had been in and out of Harvard a couple of times and had sought out many teachers and philosophers said "When I met him, I knew that he was the guy. I never try even to praise him; I don't have the words." "He unequivocally changed my life forever." "Just watching him, the way he sat (in meditation), the way he stood; we were learning by watching, by imitating. He was just there. He sort of captured all of us." Browning. (pp. 31-32)

It's rather like an ancient myth: a mature person comes from afar with an unknown practice and a charisma that together give to some young, idealistic, searching people in the 1960s an emotional home as well as a location for growth within that same practice. When Suzuki died in 1971 at the age of 67 of pancreatic cancer, Richard Baker became abbot. Richard was 33 years old, married with children, and had been for years the spearhead of a number of businesses run by the Centre which in time made it an extremely profitable enterprise. He had been practising zazen for many years, and had received Transmission from Suzuki: -- the passing-on of his teacher's dharma and lineage within the Zen tradition. He was Suzuki's heir and was accepted as such by the membership – in part because he was Suzuki's choice and in part because of his own considerable charisma. Over the next 12 years he developed his own way of being abbot. There were problems with his way that created divisions within the membership and within individual members but there was no forum within which these could be addressed.

They came to a head in 1983 when Richard was seen to quite openly have an affair with the wife of a wealthy and influential layperson, one of the core financial supporters of the Centre. The crisis occasioned by the husband's public outrage gave the Board and the Abbot's Council –many of them the same people– a space, a perceived permission to speak of and to acknowledge their hitherto unexpressed concerns and doubts about Richard's stewardship. He was asked to resign. The problems came to light over a sexual issue but equally had their roots in the extravagant life-style that Richard had assumed for himself as the head of the Centre. By comparison, the regulars, students who lived and worked at the Centre and in its multitude of businesses received a small stipend in addition to room and board.

Richard had ways of manipulation, unacknowledged even to himself most likely, to protect himself from criticism and dissent. Sex, money, power, charisma, obedience, the desire for things to be all right, a leader who cannot grasp or acknowledge his own failures and limitations, self-censorship, and the censorship perpetrated by the leader through intimidation, denial, rejection and shunning: all familiar pieces to anyone close to the centre of Therafields over the 1970s.

In the Japanese Zen tradition, the teacher is viewed as enlightened but not perfect. The teacher can make mistakes; the student needs to see these and to learn from them as things to avoid. Enlightenment or Kensho, literally means, "Having seen a corner of the nature of things," or, "Getting a glimpse of it from time to time." It's like Winacott's "good-enough mother." You do the best you can, but you can never be perfect and to try to be perfect, or to set yourself up as being perfect, is a distortion that divides you from yourself and from others. This was the missing piece for the membership at the Zen Centre over the years of Richard's stewardship. It was also the missing piece in Therafields from the days when Lea's core connection with her clients and students changed profoundly in its nature.

In both Therafields and the Zen Centre the thrust for developing the built environment came from the top, and though the motivations and forms differed, the over-all results led to a significant shift and diminution of the original praxis of both organizations. Richard Baker was not just a charismatic leader; he was also an adept businessman with an innate ability to promote and showcase his products in ways that drew not only more adherents but also wealthy and influential patrons. Even before the death of his teacher, Suzuki-Roshi, he had worked tirelessly to develop businesses that could make the nascent Zen community self-sustaining. When he assumed the position of abbot this entrepreneurial and expansive propensity became more pronounced. In time, the Zen Centre was running a bakery, a large, sea-side high-end restaurant, a store selling vegetables and other produce from the Centre's own farm, the farm itself, buildings to house the various individual adherents and often their families, and, a monastery/retreat house that catered to lay-people on holiday during the summers.

All these enterprises required an enormous amount of care. The day-to-day work was carried out by the 'students,' those who had entered the community to practice zazen – to learn about themselves in relation to the cosmos through meditation and living in the present moment. As the businesses grew and were successful, more and more labour was required to maintain them. Eventually, many of the students were spending most of their time running, for example, the restaurant or the bakery. Working a twelve-hour day left little time for meditation or instructions from their teachers. The work itself became the practice.

With Richard Baker gone, the Zen Centre went through a long and painful process to recapture its original spirit and practice. It was neither tidy nor easy. But in its wake, the Centre has carried on into the present, adhering to and teaching the lessons of its founder, Shunryu Suzuki. The closest analogue to this outcome in the sphere of Therafields is the decades-long work with new students of psychotherapy by many of Lea's original learners. The scope of the Centre for Training in Psychotherapy maintains the core importance of group and individual therapy. But importantly, it overthrows the anti-intellectualism that crept into Lea's approach, exposing its students not just to Freud, but to many of the post-Freudian writers. As that generation of workers comes to retirement, new colleagues take over and carry on a practice that had its obscure beginnings with a lady who came from England looking for a way to care for her family.

Bibliography

Downing, Michael (2001). Shoes Outside the Door: Desire, Devotion, and Excess at San Francisco Zen Centre. Counterpoint, Washington, DC.

Freud, Sigmund (1933). New Introductory Lectures on Psycho-analysis. L. and Virginia Woolf at the Hogarth Press, and the Institute of Psycho-analysis. London.

Goodbrand, Grant (2010). Therafields: The Rise and Fall of Lea Hindley-Smith's Psychoanalytic Commune. ECW Press, Toronto.

Hindley-Smith, Lea (1977). The Way It Might Have Been. Therafields Foundation, Toronto.

Janov, Arthur (1971). The primal scream: primal therapy: the cure for neurosis. Dell Publishing Company.

Lindner, Robert (1956). The Fifty Minute Hour. Bantam Books, NY.

Lowen, Alexander (1967). The Betrayal of the Body. Macmillan, NY.

Miller, Timothy (1999). The 60s Communes: Hippies and Beyond. Syracuse U Press, Syracuse, NY.

Reich, Wilhelm (1953). The Murder of Christ. The Noonday Press, NY.

Reich, Wilhelm (1973). The Cancer Biopathy. Farrar, Straus, and Giroux, NY.

Simeons, A.T.W. (1962). Man's Presumptuous Brain: An Evolutionary Interpretation of Psychosomatic Disease. EP Dutton & Co, Inc. NY.

Acknowledgements

I want to thank the many people who generously allowed me to interview them about their experiences while a part of the Therafields community. Without the input of several who had been close to Lea and her family, I would have missed many of the vital periods that marked its passage from the earliest days to the time in the early 1980s when its entire edifice was crumbling.

A number of people have read parts of the manuscript at different periods of its production, notably Dinah Forbes and Luciana Ricciutelli, giving me needed suggestions. I owe a debt of gratitude to my long time friends Maureen Jennings, Lorna Milne, Martha Jackson Pagel, Sharon MacIssac-McKenna, Bob Luker, and Maurice Farge, as well as to newer friends Kathy Honickman, Jennifer Walcott, Ellen Walters, April Boyinton Wall, Melanie Reeve, Nancy Garrow, and Roz Katz, all of whom have been helpful and encouraging.

Richard Weisman gave me considerable editorial assistance as well as unflagging enthusiasm about the manuscript, for which I will always be grateful.

I must also thank my husband, Peter von Bertoldi for his support and his expertise in the technological aspects of bringing this project to fruition.

Photographs are given by the kind permission of Andy Phillips

Andy, a constant presence at the farm

About the Author

Brenda Doyle is a proud Canadian of early Irish, Scots, and English settler heritage, who recognizes that the debt owed to Native Canadians has yet to be taken seriously and dealt with.

She was a member of the Therafields community for 17 years, later a registered psychologist in private practice, now semi-retired. She lives in Toronto with her husband enjoying connections with her two daughters, three grandchildren, and some amazing friends.